Let’s Manage Your Hard-Earned Money:

Give it Permission to Earn for You Now

Let's Manage Your Hard-Earned Money: Give it Permission to Earn for You Now

Published By: Wissira Research Lab LLC

Imprint Name: Wissira Press

US Office: Carmel, United States- 46074

India Office: KDP, RNE, India-201017

Email: editor@wissira.us, Website: https://books.wissira.us

Mobile: +91 7535 916 555

Prof. Dr. Punit Goel

Er. Niharika Singh

Dr. Subodh Sachan

Dr. K. Yogesh

ISBN - 978-93-7559-950-0

Edition: 2026

Printed In: India

Let's Manage Your Hard-Earned Money:

Give it Permission to Earn for You Now

2026

Authors:

Prof. Dr. Punit Goel

Er. Niharika Singh

Dr. Subodh Sachan

Dr. K. Yogesh

Published By

Wissira Research Lab

ISBN 978-93-7559-950-0

9 789375 599500

Preface

Money is one of the most powerful tools in our lives-yet it is also one of the least formally taught subjects. We spend years learning how to earn, but very little time learning how to manage, multiply, and protect what we earn. As a result, many hardworking individuals find themselves constantly busy, constantly earning, yet not steadily building wealth. This book was written to change that pattern.

Let's Manage Your Hard-Earned Money: Give It Permission to Earn for You Now is not about complicated financial jargon or risky shortcuts. It is about clarity. It is about shifting the focus from working endlessly for money to allowing money to begin working for you. The core philosophy is simple: income sustains life, but assets create freedom.

Throughout these chapters, you will explore your personal money story, understand the psychology behind financial decisions, and design a practical blueprint for budgeting and investing. You will learn why an emergency fund is more powerful than high returns, why compounding rewards patience, and why diversification protects progress. You will also discover how multiple income streams and smart tax planning can accelerate your journey toward financial independence.

This book does not promise instant wealth. Instead, it offers something far more valuable-financial confidence. Each chapter builds step by step, transforming abstract ideas into measurable strategies. Whether you are at the beginning of your financial journey or refining an existing plan, the principles shared here are designed to be timeless and adaptable.

Your hard-earned money represents your time, effort, skill, and sacrifice. It deserves thoughtful direction. When managed intentionally, it becomes more than currency-it becomes a partner in your future.

Now is the moment to stop working only for money.
It is time to give your money permission to earn for you.

Overview of the Book

Let's Manage Your Hard-Earned Money: Give It Permission to Earn for You Now is a practical, structured guide designed to help individuals transform their relationship with money-from earning and spending to building and multiplying. The book moves beyond motivational advice and provides a clear financial roadmap rooted in discipline, awareness, and strategic action.

The journey begins with understanding your financial identity. Before managing money effectively, one must recognize the psychological patterns and habits that influence decisions. By examining mindset, behaviour, and personal beliefs, the book lays a strong foundation for long-term financial clarity.

From there, it challenges a common misconception: income does not equal wealth. Through structured budgeting methods and intentional allocation strategies, readers learn how to convert earnings into assets. The book emphasizes financial resilience through emergency funds and insurance planning before exploring the power of compounding and disciplined investing.

As the chapters progress, the focus shifts toward growth-diversified investing, multiple income streams, tax efficiency, and wealth protection. The final section presents a measurable blueprint for financial freedom, helping readers calculate their "freedom number" and design a transition from active income to asset income.

This book is suitable for salaried professionals, entrepreneurs, students, and anyone seeking structured financial control. Whether starting from zero or refining an existing plan, the principles presented here are practical, adaptable, and designed for sustainable wealth creation.

In essence, this is not just a finance book-it is a step-by-step guide to turning effort into assets and earnings into enduring financial security.

Table of Contents

1
Your Money Story – Understanding Your Financial Identity

1.1 The Psychology Behind Your Financial Decisions

Money decisions are rarely mathematical alone; they are deeply emotional. From childhood, individuals absorb financial patterns-how parents saved, spent, or discussed money. These experiences form subconscious beliefs such as "money is scarce," "money is hard to earn," or "money is meant to be enjoyed immediately."
Financial behaviour is shaped long before we open our first bank account. During childhood, we observe how money is handled in our homes: whether it is discussed openly or treated as a source of tension, whether it is saved cautiously or spent freely. These early experiences quietly form what psychologists call "money scripts" - internal beliefs about wealth, security, success, and worth.

For example, a child who grows up hearing "we can't afford that" may internalize scarcity, even if they later earn well. Another who sees money used to reward emotions may associate spending with comfort or celebration. These beliefs operate subconsciously and often guide adult decisions without deliberate awareness.

Behavioural finance research consistently shows that humans are not fully rational decision-makers. Emotions such as fear, overconfidence, anxiety, pride, and social comparison influence financial actions. During market downturns, fear can trigger panic-selling even when long-term fundamentals remain strong. Conversely, during bull markets, greed or overconfidence may encourage excessive risk-taking.

Stress is another major driver. Many individuals spend impulsively to regulate emotions - retail therapy after a difficult day, luxury purchases to signal status, or avoidance of financial planning due to anxiety. These patterns are less about money itself and more about emotional coping.

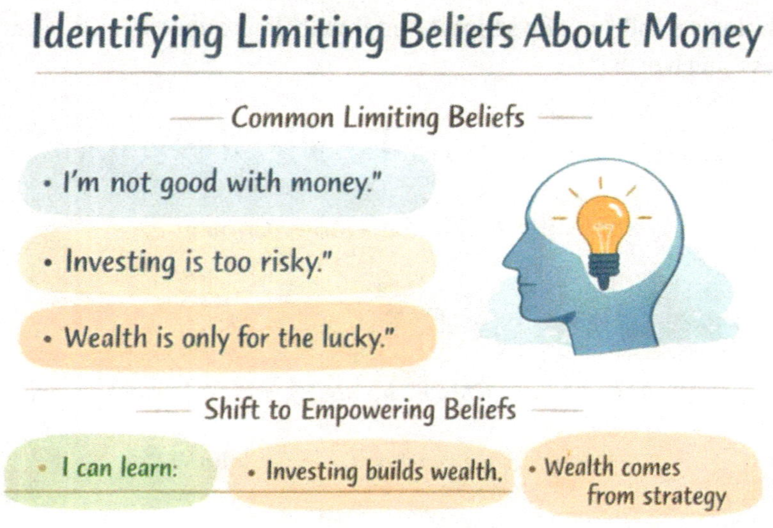

Recognizing these emotional triggers is transformative. When you pause to ask, "Am I acting from strategy or from emotion?" you begin shifting from reactive behaviour to intentional financial management. This self-awareness creates space between feeling and action - and that space is where financial discipline grows.

True financial maturity does not start with spreadsheets. It starts with understanding your emotional relationship with money. Once you identify the psychological patterns influencing your choices, you can redesign them consciously - replacing fear-driven decisions with structured planning, and impulsive reactions with long-term vision.

Money follows mindset more than mathematics.

1.2 Identifying Limiting Beliefs About Money

Many people unknowingly carry limiting beliefs that restrict wealth creation. Statements like "I am not good with money," "Investing is risky," or "Wealth is only for the lucky" silently shape behaviour. These beliefs can prevent individuals from learning about investing, negotiating salaries, or exploring opportunities.

Limiting beliefs about money are often invisible because they feel like facts rather than opinions. Phrases such as "I'm just not good with numbers," "Investing is basically gambling," or "Rich people are different from people like us" quietly shape financial behaviour over time. These beliefs are rarely questioned because they are absorbed from family, culture, media, or early experiences.

The problem is not the statement itself - it's the behaviour it produces.

If someone believes they are "bad with money," they may avoid budgeting altogether. If they think investing is dangerous, they may leave their savings idle, losing long-term growth opportunities. If wealth is viewed as luck-based, effort toward financial education may feel pointless. Over time, avoidance reinforces the belief, creating a self-fulfilling cycle.

Limiting beliefs also affect confidence in earning. Many professionals hesitate to negotiate salaries, raise prices, or ask for promotions because they subconsciously feel they are "not worth more." That internal narrative can silently cap income growth far below potential.

Breaking these patterns begins with awareness. Ask:

- What did I hear about money growing up?
- What do I believe wealthy people are like?
- Do I feel guilt, fear, or discomfort around earning more?

Once identified, beliefs can be reframed. Instead of "I'm not good with money," shift to "Financial management is a skill that improves with practice." Instead of "Investing is risky," consider "Not learning how to invest carries its own risk." These are not empty affirmations; they are cognitive rewrites grounded in personal agency.

Over time, repeated empowering beliefs reshape identity. When you begin to see yourself as someone capable of learning, managing, and growing wealth, your actions align accordingly. You seek knowledge. You plan. You stay disciplined.

Wealth creation starts in the mind long before it appears in the bank account. Change the belief - and behaviour follows.

Limiting Belief	Underlying Psychological Pattern	Behavioural Impact	Empowering Replacement Belief	Expected Positive Outcome
"I am not good with money."	Fixed mindset; fear of failure	Avoids budgeting, investing, financial learning	"Money management is a skill I can learn."	Increased financial literacy and confidence
"Investing is too risky."	Loss aversion; fear-based thinking	Keeps savings idle; misses growth opportunities	"Calculated investing builds long-term wealth."	Structured portfolio building and disciplined investing

"Wealth is only for lucky people."	External locus of control	Low motivation to plan or strategize	"Wealth grows through discipline and informed decisions."	Active financial planning and opportunity seeking
"Talking about money is uncomfortable."	Social conditioning; emotional discomfort	Avoids salary negotiation or financial discussions	"Open money conversations create better opportunities."	Improved negotiation and financial clarity
"If I earn more, people will judge me."	Social comparison; fear of rejection	Self-sabotages growth opportunities	"Financial growth does not diminish my values."	Greater ambition and income expansion
"I don't earn enough to invest."	Scarcity mindset	Delays investing; consumes entire income	"Even small amounts invested consistently grow over time."	Habit-based investing and compounding benefits

1.3 Financial Habits: The Invisible Drivers of Wealth

Daily habits determine long-term financial outcomes. Small, repeated actions-tracking expenses, saving first, reviewing investments quarterly-compound over time. Conversely, ignoring bills, accumulating credit card debt, or postponing planning can quietly erode financial stability. Habits operate automatically, which makes them powerful. By creating structured systems-automatic savings transfers, fixed investment schedules, goal-based budgeting-you reduce decision fatigue and strengthen positive money behaviour.

Financial success is rarely the result of a single brilliant investment or sudden windfall. It is typically the outcome of consistent, repeated behaviours sustained over years. Daily habits-often small and seemingly insignificant-shape long-term financial stability through the power of compounding.

For example, regularly tracking expenses increases awareness. Awareness improves control. Control improves decision-making. Similarly, saving before spending-even a modest percentage of income-creates a discipline that gradually builds financial resilience. Over time, these small actions accumulate into meaningful assets.

On the other hand, negative habits operate just as quietly. Ignoring monthly statements, making minimum credit card payments, delaying retirement planning, or frequently making impulsive purchases may not feel damaging in the short term. However, when repeated over months and years, they erode wealth through interest costs, missed investment growth, and financial stress.

The reason habits are so influential is that they function automatically. Once a behaviour becomes routine, it requires minimal mental effort. This can either work in your favour or against you. If your default behaviour is to invest automatically, review financial goals quarterly, and maintain an emergency fund, wealth-building becomes almost effortless. If your default is avoidance or impulsive spending, financial instability becomes the pattern.

This is where structured systems become powerful. Automation reduces reliance on willpower. Automatic savings transfers ensure consistency. Scheduled investments remove emotional timing decisions. Goal-based budgeting gives direction to spending instead of restriction.

In essence, habits remove emotion from execution. Instead of deciding every month whether to save, invest, or plan-you create a system that does it for you.

Wealth is not a product of motivation. It is a product of well-designed habits repeated long enough to compound.

Table: Positive vs. Negative Financial Habits and Their Long-Term Impact

Financial Habit	Type	Short-Term Effect	Long-Term Impact	System-Based Solution
Saving a fixed percentage of income first	Positive	Slight reduction in immediate spending	Strong emergency fund and investment growth	Automatic salary-to-savings transfer
Tracking monthly expenses	Positive	Increased awareness	Improved budgeting and reduced waste	Expense-tracking app or monthly review routine
Quarterly portfolio review	Positive	Time commitment	Optimized investment allocation	Calendar-based financial review reminder
Paying only minimum credit card dues	Negative	Short-term cash relief	High interest burden and debt accumulation	Automated full-bill payment setup
Impulsive online purchases	Negative	Temporary emotional satisfaction	Erosion of savings	24-hour pause rule before non-essential purchases

Postponing retirement planning	Negative	Immediate comfort	Reduced compounding benefits	SIP or recurring retirement investment plan
Maintaining an emergency fund	Positive	Delayed discretionary spending	Financial security during crises	Separate high-liquidity emergency account

1.4 Rewriting Your Financial Identity

Once awareness develops, transformation becomes possible. Rewriting your financial identity involves setting clear goals, defining values, and committing to disciplined action.
Instead of seeing yourself as a spender, you become a wealth builder. Instead of surviving month-to-month, you plan for long-term security.

This shift is not about overnight change but consistent improvement. When identity changes, behaviour follows naturally, and financial progress becomes sustainable rather than temporary.

Financial transformation does not begin with a new investment account or a higher income. It begins with a shift in identity. Identity answers the deeper question: *"Who am I when it comes to money?"* If you see yourself as careless, unlucky, or perpetually struggling, your behaviour will unconsciously reinforce that narrative. But when you redefine yourself as disciplined, capable, and growth-oriented, your actions begin aligning with that version.

Rewriting your financial identity starts with clarity. You must define what financial success means personally-not socially. Is it freedom from debt? Long-term security? Generational wealth? Flexibility to pursue passion? Clear goals provide direction, and direction shapes daily decisions.

Values play an equally important role. If financial growth aligns with your core values-stability, family security, independence, contribution-it becomes meaningful rather than burdensome. Saving and investing stop feeling restrictive and start feeling purposeful.

This shift is gradual, not dramatic. Identity changes through consistent evidence. When you track expenses monthly, you reinforce the identity of being responsible. When you invest systematically, you reinforce the identity of being strategic. When you plan long-term, you reinforce the identity of being forward-thinking.

Instead of labelling yourself as "a spender," you begin saying, "I am someone who manages money wisely." Instead of living month-to-month, you adopt systems that prioritize future stability.

Sustainable financial progress occurs when behaviour is driven by identity rather than motivation. Motivation fluctuates. Identity endures. Once you internalize the belief that you are a wealth builder, financial discipline becomes natural rather than forced.

You don’t just manage money differently. You become someone different with money.

Table: From Old Identity to New Financial Identity

Old Financial Identity	Associated Behaviour	New Financial Identity	Reinforcing Actions	Long-Term Result
“I am bad with money.”	Avoids budgeting	“I am learning to manage money wisely.”	Monthly expense tracking	Increased financial control
“I always struggle financially.”	Lives paycheck to paycheck	“I build stability step by step.”	Emergency fund creation	Reduced financial stress

"I am a spender."	Impulsive purchases	"I am a disciplined investor."	Automatic monthly investment	Wealth accumulation
"Planning is overwhelming."	Avoids long-term goals	"I plan with clarity and patience."	Annual financial goal review	Structured financial growth
"Money controls me."	Emotional financial decisions	"I make intentional financial choices."	Pre-planned budget allocation	Sustainable financial independence

2

Income Is Not Wealth – Breaking the Paycheck Illusion

2.1 Understanding the Difference Between Income and Assets

Income is the money you earn; wealth is the assets you own that generate income. A high salary may support a comfortable lifestyle, but without savings and investments, it does not create financial independence. Assets such as stocks, bonds, rental properties, or business equity produce cash flow even when you are not actively working. Wealth grows when money is directed toward acquiring assets rather than funding lifestyle upgrades.

Many people assume that earning more automatically makes them wealthy. It doesn't. Income and assets are related, but they are not the same thing-and confusing them is one of the biggest financial mistakes people make.

Income is the money you receive for your effort, time, or services. It may come from a salary, business profits, consulting fees, or freelance work. Income requires ongoing activity. If you stop working, the income often stops too. Even a very high salary mainly supports expenses-rent or EMIs, travel, lifestyle choices, school fees, and daily living costs. Income provides comfort, but by itself, it does not guarantee long-term security.

Assets, on the other hand, are things you own that generate value or produce additional income. Examples include stocks that pay dividends, bonds that earn interest, rental properties that provide monthly rent, or ownership in a business that distributes profits. Unlike income, assets can continue generating cash flow even when you are not actively working. This is the foundation of financial independence.

The key difference lies in sustainability. Income is active; assets are productive. Income pays the bills. Assets build wealth.

True wealth grows when a portion of earned income is consistently redirected into acquiring assets. Instead of increasing lifestyle spending every time income rises, financially disciplined individuals invest surplus earnings into appreciating or income-generating instruments. Over time, these assets begin to produce their own cash flow, creating a compounding effect.

For example, a professional earning ₹20 lakhs annually but spending nearly all of it may appear affluent but remains financially dependent on continued employment. In contrast, someone earning ₹10 lakhs but consistently investing 30–40% into diversified assets may gradually build a portfolio that eventually covers living expenses.

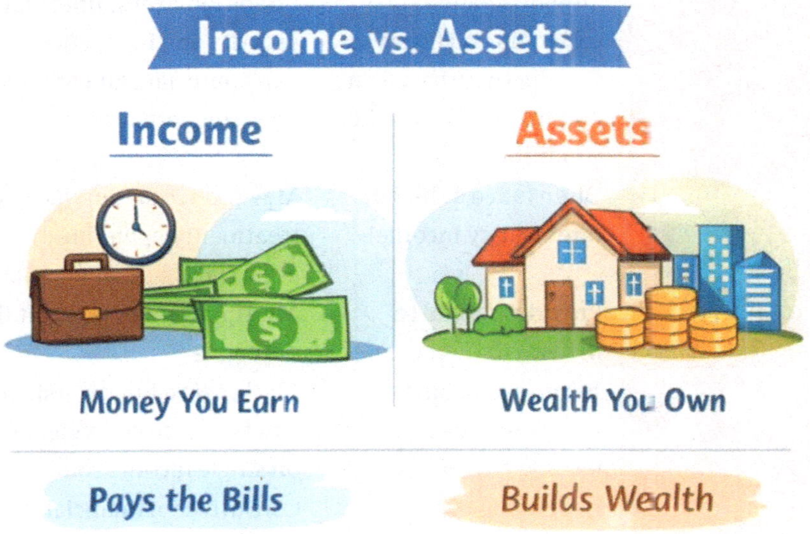

In simple terms:

- Income gives you purchasing power.
- Assets give you freedom.

Wealth is not measured by how much you earn, but by how long your assets can support your life without requiring your daily labour.

Basis of Comparison	Income	Assets
Definition	Money earned from active work, services, or business operations	Resources owned that generate value or income over time
Nature	Active and effort-dependent	Passive or semi-passive wealth-generating
Source	Salary, wages, consulting fees, business profits	Stocks, bonds, rental property, business equity, intellectual property
Dependency on Work	Stops when work stops (in most cases)	Can continue generating income without daily effort
Purpose	Supports daily expenses and lifestyle	Builds long-term financial security and independence
Stability	Can fluctuate based on employment or market conditions	Can appreciate and provide recurring returns
Tax Treatment	Often taxed at higher rates (salary income)	May receive favourable tax treatment depending on asset class
Role in Wealth Creation	Provides capital to invest	Multiplies invested capital over time
Risk Factor	Job loss or business slowdown affects income directly	Market risk, but diversified assets reduce dependency on single income source
Financial Freedom Impact	Limited unless converted into investments	Core driver of financial independence

2.2 Lifestyle Inflation: The Silent Wealth Killer

As income increases, expenses often rise proportionally. Bigger homes, upgraded cars, premium subscriptions-these changes feel like progress but may limit wealth accumulation.

Lifestyle inflation is subtle. Instead of saving raises or bonuses, many expand spending patterns. Over time, financial dependence grows despite higher earnings. Controlling lifestyle inflation allows income growth to translate into asset growth.

Lifestyle inflation happens when spending rises along with income. It often feels natural-after all, if you earn more, why not enjoy more? The problem is not improvement in lifestyle; the problem is automatic expansion without intentional investing.

When salaries increase, many people upgrade their homes, switch to more expensive cars, dine out more frequently, subscribe to premium services, or adopt costlier habits. Each individual upgrade seems reasonable. Collectively, however, they absorb most of the additional income that could have been invested.

The danger lies in how subtle this process is. A ₹20,000 monthly raise does not feel dramatic. But if that raise is fully redirected into EMI increases, lifestyle subscriptions, and recurring expenses, the long-term impact becomes significant. Over years, higher fixed costs create greater financial dependency. Even a high earner may feel financially stretched because expenses have permanently adjusted upward.

Lifestyle inflation delays wealth creation because surplus income-the fuel for investment-shrinks. Without surplus, asset accumulation slows or stops. As a result, despite earning more, net worth grows slowly.

The goal is not to live minimally forever. It is to upgrade strategically. When assets begin generating cash flow, lifestyle improvements become sustainable rather than fragile.

In simple terms:

- Uncontrolled lifestyle inflation increases financial pressure.
- Controlled lifestyle choices increase financial freedom.

Wealth grows not when income rises-but when expenses rise slower than income.

Table: Impact of Lifestyle Inflation on Wealth Growth

Scenario	Income Increase	Additional Spending	Investment Allocation	Long-Term Effect
Uncontrolled Inflation	₹20,000/month raise	₹18,000/month lifestyle upgrade	₹2,000/month	Slow asset growth, higher dependency
Balanced Approach	₹20,000/month raise	₹8,000/month upgrade	₹12,000/month	Moderate asset accumulation
Disciplined Growth Strategy	₹20,000/month raise	₹5,000/month upgrade	₹15,000/month	Strong compounding and faster financial independence

Case Study: The Trap of Lifestyle Inflation vs Strategic Wealth Building

Background

Rahul and Arjun graduated from the same university and began working in the same industry. Both started with an annual salary of ₹8,00,000. Over the next 8 years, their income steadily increased to ₹20,00,000 per year due to promotions and performance bonuses.

Despite earning the same income trajectory, their financial outcomes were drastically different.

Rahul: The Lifestyle Upgrade Path

Each time Rahul received a raise, he upgraded his lifestyle:

- Moved to a larger apartment

- Purchased a new car on EMI
- Increased dining, travel, and subscription spending
- Opted for premium gadgets and luxury memberships

On average, he saved only 5–8% of his income annually. Most bonuses were spent on vacations or lifestyle upgrades.

After 8 years:

- High monthly fixed expenses
- Limited investment portfolio
- Heavy EMI commitments
- Net worth: Approximately ₹12–15 lakhs

Despite earning ₹20,00,000 annually, Rahul felt financially stretched. A job disruption would significantly affect his stability.

Arjun: The Asset Accumulation Strategy

Arjun also improved his lifestyle-but selectively. With each raise:

- He increased investments first
- Directed 35–40% of income toward mutual funds, equities, and retirement plans
- Purchased one rental property using disciplined savings
- Avoided unnecessary recurring lifestyle costs

He allowed only a modest portion of income increases to upgrade his living standard.

After 8 years:

- Diversified investment portfolio
- Rental income covering 25% of living expenses

- Low debt exposure
- Net worth: Approximately ₹85–95 lakhs

Arjun's assets began generating income, reducing his dependence on his salary.

Financial Comparison Table (After 8 Years)

Parameter	Rahul (Lifestyle Inflation)	Arjun (Controlled Lifestyle)
Final Annual Income	₹20,00,000	₹20,00,000
Savings Rate	5–8%	35–40%
Investment Portfolio	Limited	Diversified & growing
Passive Income	None	Rental + dividends
EMI Burden	High	Moderate
Estimated Net Worth	₹12–15 Lakhs	₹85–95 Lakhs
Financial Stress Level	High	Low
Dependency on Job	Very High	Reduced

Key Insight

Both individuals earned the same income. The difference was not earning power-it was spending behaviour.

Lifestyle inflation made Rahul income-rich but asset-poor.

Controlled lifestyle growth made Arjun income-smart and asset-strong.

Core Lesson

Income growth does not automatically create wealth.
If expenses expand at the same pace as income, financial dependence

increases.
When income growth is partially redirected toward assets, wealth compounds over time.

2.3 Cash Flow Management: The Foundation of Financial Control

Cash flow represents the movement of money in and out of your life. Positive cash flow-earning more than you spend-creates room for saving and investing.
Tracking income streams and categorizing expenses reveal financial leaks. Small recurring costs can accumulate into substantial yearly amounts. Conscious cash flow management ensures surplus funds are directed toward investments rather than unplanned consumption.

Cash flow is the rhythm of your financial life. It reflects how money enters and exits your system-salary credits, business income, dividends on one side: rent, EMIs, utilities, groceries, subscriptions, and discretionary spending on the other.

Many people focus on income levels but ignore cash flow patterns. Yet financial control does not begin with earning more-it begins with managing what already flows through your hands.

Positive cash flow occurs when total income exceeds total expenses. This surplus becomes the fuel for savings, investing, and wealth creation. Without surplus, even a high-income individual may remain financially stagnant.

The real power of cash flow management lies in awareness. When income streams are tracked and expenses categorized, financial blind spots become visible. For example:

- Multiple digital subscriptions
- Impulse online purchases
- Frequent food delivery
- Underused memberships

- Unplanned lifestyle upgrades

Individually, these seem minor. Collectively, they can drain significant amounts annually.

For instance, ₹3,000 per month in unnoticed recurring expenses equals ₹36,000 annually. Invested at a reasonable return, this amount could compound meaningfully over time. What feels small in a month becomes substantial over a decade.

Cash flow management involves three core actions:

1. Tracking income sources (salary, side income, dividends)
2. Categorizing expenses (fixed, variable, discretionary)
3. Redirecting surplus toward asset-building investments

The goal is not restriction-it is intentional direction. When cash flow is consciously managed, money serves long-term priorities instead of temporary impulses.

In simple terms:

- Income determines your earning capacity.

- Cash flow determines your financial discipline.
- Surplus determines your wealth potential.

Mastering cash flow is the foundation upon which every investment strategy stands.

Table: Structure of Personal Cash Flow

Component	Description	Example
Income Sources	Money received regularly or irregularly	Salary, freelance income, dividends
Fixed Expenses	Mandatory recurring costs	Rent/EMI insurance premiums, utilities
Variable Expenses	Fluctuating lifestyle expenses	Groceries, fuel, entertainment
Discretionary Spending	Non-essential spending	Dining out, subscriptions, shopping
Net Cash Flow	Income minus total expenses	Surplus or deficit amount
Surplus Allocation	Portion directed toward investments	Mutual funds, stocks, retirement plans

Mini Case Example

Priya earns ₹1,20,000 per month. Her monthly expenses total ₹1,05,000.

At first glance, she assumes she is "doing fine." But after categorizing expenses, she discovers ₹12,000 in avoidable discretionary spending. By reducing this to ₹6,000 and investing the difference:

- Monthly investment increases by ₹6,000
- Annual investment increase: ₹72,000
- Over 10 years (with compounding), this creates significant wealth

This small correction transforms cash flow into capital growth.

2.4 Building Wealth Through Intentional Allocation

Wealth is built through deliberate allocation of money. A structured approach may include dividing income into essentials, savings, investments, and personal enjoyment.
The key principle is "pay yourself first." By prioritizing investment contributions before discretionary spending, wealth becomes systematic. Intentional allocation transforms earnings into financial growth rather than temporary comfort.

Wealth does not grow accidentally. It grows when money is directed with purpose. Intentional allocation means deciding in advance where each portion of your income will go-before emotions, impulses, or lifestyle temptations take over.

Many individuals earn well but allocate randomly. Expenses come first, then whatever remains may or may not be saved. This reactive approach makes wealth creation inconsistent. In contrast, structured allocation makes it predictable.

A practical framework involves dividing income into four broad categories:

1. **Essentials** – housing, utilities, food, transportation, insurance

2. **Savings & Emergency Fund** – liquidity for financial stability
3. **Investments** – equity funds, retirement accounts business assets, real estate
4. **Personal Enjoyment** – travel, hobbies, lifestyle upgrades

The philosophy behind this structure is simple: money must serve both present needs and future security.

The most powerful principle within intentional allocation is **"pay yourself first."** Instead of saving what remains after spending, you invest first and spend what remains. Investment contributions are treated like non-negotiable obligations-similar to rent or EMIs.

For example, if someone earns ₹1,00,000 monthly and commits 30% to investments immediately, ₹30,000 is allocated before lifestyle decisions are made. This removes reliance on willpower. Wealth becomes automated.

Intentional allocation creates discipline without requiring constant sacrifice. It ensures that income growth translates into asset growth. Over time, consistent allocation builds momentum through compounding, gradually shifting financial dependence away from active income toward asset-generated income.

In essence:

- Random spending creates temporary comfort.
- Structured allocation creates long-term freedom.

Wealth is not built by how much you earn-but by how consistently you assign your earnings toward productive assets.

Table: Example of Intentional Allocation Model

Category	Allocation %	Monthly Amount (₹1,00,000 Income)	Purpose
Essentials	40%	₹40,000	Core living expenses
Savings (Emergency Fund)	10%	₹10,000	Financial stability buffer
Investments	30%	₹30,000	Wealth-building assets
Personal Enjoyment	15%	₹15,000	Lifestyle satisfaction
Skill Development	5%	₹5,000	Future income growth

Mini Case Example

Neha earns ₹15,00,000 annually. Earlier, she saved irregularly. After adopting intentional allocation:

- 35% Automatically invested each month
- Emergency fund built within 18 months
- Discretionary spending kept within 15%

Within 6 years, her investments began generating dividend and interest income that covered 20% of her living expenses.

The transformation was not due to higher income-but due to structured allocation.

3

Budgeting with Purpose – Designing a Money Blueprint

3.1 Budgeting as a Strategy, Not a Restriction

Many views budgeting as limiting freedom. In reality, budgeting provides clarity and control. It is not about eliminating joy but aligning spending with priorities.
A purposeful budget reflects personal values-education, travel, security, family, entrepreneurship. When spending matches intention, guilt reduces and confidence increases.

Budgeting is often misunderstood as a rigid system that prevents enjoyment or spontaneity. Many people associate it with cutting expenses, saying "no" to desires, or constantly worrying about money. However, budgeting is better understood as a strategic tool that brings awareness and direction to financial decisions. Rather than limiting freedom, it actually creates a framework within which informed and confident choices can be made.

At its core, budgeting is about intentional allocation. Every individual has limited financial resources, but unlimited desires. Without a plan, money tends to flow toward immediate gratification-impulse purchases, unplanned subscriptions, or lifestyle inflation. Over time, this can lead to stress, debt, or missed opportunities. A structured budget, on the other hand, ensures that essential expenses, savings, and long-term goals are prioritized before discretionary spending occurs. This approach strengthens financial stability instead of restricting enjoyment.

A well-designed budget is deeply personal. It should reflect individual values and aspirations. For one person, education and skill development may be the top priority. For another, travel experiences, supporting family, building a business, or early retirement may matter most. When a budget mirrors these priorities, spending becomes purposeful. Money is no longer spent randomly; it is directed toward what truly matters. This alignment reduces financial guilt because purchases are intentional rather than impulsive.

Budgeting also increases psychological confidence. When individuals know exactly where their money is going, uncertainty decreases. They can anticipate upcoming expenses, prepare for emergencies, and track progress toward financial goals. This clarity creates a sense of control, which is essential for long-term financial well-being. Instead of feeling anxious about whether there will be enough money at the end of the month, a person with a clear budget operates with awareness and planning.

Importantly, budgeting does not eliminate joy. It simply assigns space for it. Entertainment, hobbies, dining out, or vacations can and should be included as dedicated categories within the financial plan. When enjoyment is planned rather than accidental, it becomes sustainable. The individual can spend on leisure without fear because the essential obligations have already been covered.

In essence, budgeting transforms money from a source of stress into a strategic resource. It encourages disciplined decision-making while preserving flexibility. By aligning spending with values and long-term goals, budgeting empowers individuals to live intentionally rather than reactively.

Aspect	Budget as a Restriction (Common Misconception)	Budget as a Strategy (Reality)	Impact on Individual
Financial Control	Feels limiting and rigid	Provides clarity and structured decision-making	Greater confidence and reduced anxiety
Spending Behaviour	Focused on cutting expenses only	Focused on intentional	Purpose-driven spending

		allocation of money	
Emotional Experience	Creates guilt around spending	Encourages mindful and planned enjoyment	Reduced financial guilt
Alignment with Values	Money spent impulsively	Spending reflects priorities (education, travel, family, business)	Stronger sense of fulfilment
Long-Term Planning	Short-term reaction to expenses	Supports savings, investments, and goal tracking	Improved financial stability
Freedom	Perceived loss of freedom	Enables informed and conscious choices	Sustainable lifestyle balance
Risk Management	No preparation for emergencies	Includes emergency funds and safety buffers	Increased financial resilience
Decision-Making	Reactive and emotional	Proactive and strategic	Better financial discipline

3.2 Popular Budgeting Frameworks and Their Applications

Several structured budgeting systems help individuals manage finances effectively:

- 50-30-20 Rule: 50% needs, 30% wants, 20% savings/investments.
- Zero-Based Budgeting: Every rupee assigned a purpose.
- Envelope Method: Physical or digital allocation of spending categories.

Each framework offers flexibility. The best method is one that fits lifestyle and income patterns. The objective is consistency, not perfection.

Structured budgeting frameworks provide individuals with systematic ways to organize income and control spending. While personal finance principles remain universal-spend wisely, save consistently, and invest strategically-the method used to implement these principles can vary depending on income level, lifestyle, financial goals, and personality. The purpose of a budgeting framework is not rigidity, but discipline with flexibility.

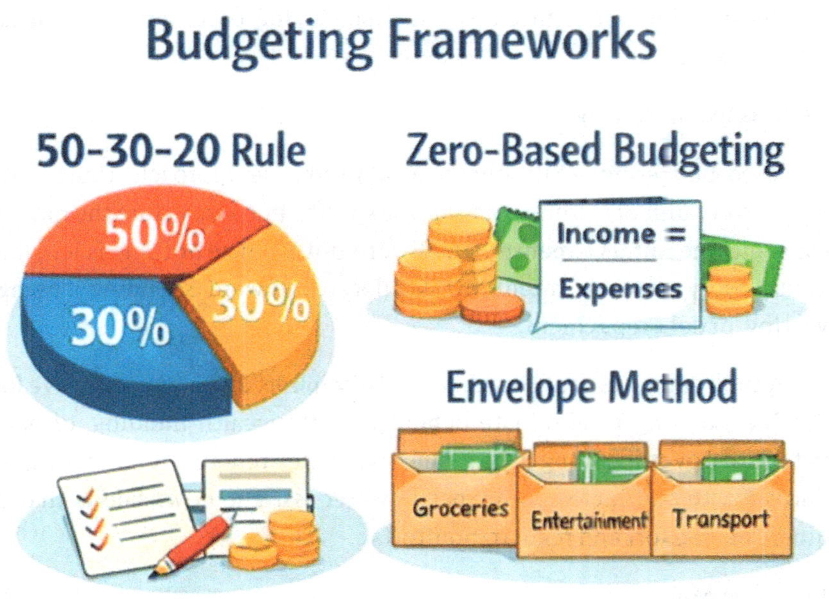

1. 50-30-20 Rule

The 50-30-20 rule is one of the simplest and most widely accepted budgeting models. It divides net income into three broad categories:

- 50% for essential needs (rent, groceries, utilities, insurance, transportation)
- 30% for discretionary wants (dining out, entertainment, travel, hobbies)
- 20% for savings and investments (emergency fund, retirement, SIPs, debt repayment)

This method works particularly well for salaried individuals who prefer a straightforward allocation system without detailed tracking of every transaction. Its strength lies in balance-it ensures that lifestyle enjoyment and long-term security are both included in financial planning. However, it may require adjustment in cities with high living costs where essential expenses exceed 50%.

2. Zero-Based Budgeting

Zero-based budgeting (ZBB) follows a more precise approach. Under this system, every unit of income is assigned a specific purpose before the month begins. Income minus expenses equals zero-not because nothing is left, but because every rupee is intentionally allocated toward spending, saving, investing, or debt repayment.

This method demands active tracking and discipline. It is highly effective for individuals aiming to eliminate debt, accelerate wealth building, or gain strict control over spending habits. Since no money remains "unassigned," it reduces waste and increases financial awareness. The downside is that it requires more effort and regular monitoring.

3. Envelope Method

The envelope method is a tangible way of managing discretionary spending. Traditionally, cash is placed into labelled envelopes such as groceries, entertainment, transport, and shopping. Once the envelope is empty, spending in that category stops for the month. In modern applications, digital wallets or budgeting apps replicate this system virtually.

This approach is especially useful for people who struggle with overspending. It creates visible limits and strengthens spending discipline. While highly effective for controlling variable expenses, it may not be practical for all fixed or automated payments.

Choosing the Right Framework

No single budgeting model is universally superior. The most effective framework is the one that aligns with an individual's income pattern, financial complexity, and behavioural tendencies. A salaried professional may benefit from the 50-30-20 structure, an entrepreneur with fluctuating income may prefer zero-based planning, and someone working on spending control might find the envelope method transformative.

Ultimately, consistency matters more than perfection. A simple system applied regularly will outperform a complex system applied occasionally. The goal is sustainable financial discipline-not rigid financial restriction.

Comparative Table: Budgeting Frameworks and Applications

Framework	Core Principle	Best Suited For	Advantages	Limitations
50-30-20 Rule	Percentage-based allocation of income	Salaried individuals seeking simplicity	Easy to follow, balanced lifestyle approach	May not fit high-cost living areas
Zero-Based Budgeting	Every rupee assigned a purpose	Debt reduction, wealth acceleration, disciplined planners	Maximizes control and awareness	Requires detailed tracking and time
Envelope Method	Fixed spending limits per category	Individuals prone to overspending	Strong spending discipline, visual control	Less flexible for digital/automated payments

3.3 Aligning Budget with Short-Term and Long-Term Goals

Budgeting becomes powerful when tied to goals. Short-term goals may include building an emergency fund or paying off debt. Long-term goals may include home ownership, retirement planning, or financial freedom.

When goals are quantified-with timelines and amounts-they provide direction. Instead of vague saving intentions, you build measurable progress milestones.

Budgeting gains real strength when it is linked to clearly defined financial objectives. Without goals, saving becomes vague and inconsistent. With goals, every allocation has purpose. A budget is not just about tracking expenses-it is about directing resources toward meaningful outcomes.

Short-Term Goals

Short-term financial goals typically span from a few months to three years. These may include:

- Building an emergency fund (3–6 months of expenses)
- Paying off credit card or personal loan debt
- Saving for a certification, travel plan, or business startup capital

These goals create financial stability. For example, an emergency fund reduces dependence on loans during unexpected events such as medical expenses or job interruptions. When a person assigns a fixed monthly amount toward this goal, progress becomes visible and motivating.

Instead of saying, "I should save more," the budget now reflects: ₹10,000 per month toward emergency fund → Target ₹3,00,000 → Timeline 30 months.

Clarity replaces uncertainty.

Long-Term Goals

Long-term goals extend over several years or decades. These often include:

- Home ownership
- Children's education planning
- Retirement corpus creation

- Achieving financial independence

Such goals require structured saving and disciplined investing. Because they involve large sums, they must be broken into manageable milestones. A retirement goal of ₹3 crore may feel overwhelming-but when converted into monthly SIP contributions with expected return assumptions, it becomes actionable.

Long-term budgeting integrates compounding, inflation planning, and periodic review. This transforms dreams into calculated financial strategies.

The Power of Quantification

Goals become effective only when they are:

1. **Specific** – Clearly defined purpose
2. **Measurable** – Fixed amount required
3. **Time-bound** – Defined timeline
4. **Realistic** – Based on income capacity
5. **Reviewable** – Periodically evaluated

When goals are quantified, your budget becomes a performance dashboard. Each month reflects progress. Each year reflects growth. This measurable advancement builds confidence and discipline.

Vague intention creates delay. Quantified planning creates momentum.

Table: Linking Budget Allocation to Goals

Goal Type	Example Goal	Target Amount	Timeline	Monthly Allocation Strategy
Short-Term	Emergency Fund	₹3,00,000	24–30 months	Allocate fixed monthly savings before

				discretionary spending
Short-Term	Debt Repayment	₹1,20,000	12 months	Prioritize high-interest repayment in budget
Long-Term	Home Purchase	₹20,00,000 (down payment)	5 years	Invest in diversified instruments with growth potential
Long-Term	Retirement Corpus	₹3 crore	25–30 years	Monthly SIP + annual increment adjustments

3.4 Automation and Technology in Budget Management

Modern tools simplify budgeting. Banking apps, expense trackers, and automated investment platforms reduce manual effort. Automation ensures consistency-monthly SIPs, scheduled transfers, recurring savings deposits. Technology minimizes emotional interference and enhances discipline. When systems operate

automatically, financial growth continues even during busy or stressful periods.

In today's digital economy, budgeting no longer requires manual ledger entries or constant calculations. Technology has transformed personal finance management by making tracking, saving, and investing more efficient and consistent. Modern financial tools reduce friction, eliminate guesswork, and help individuals stay aligned with their financial plans.

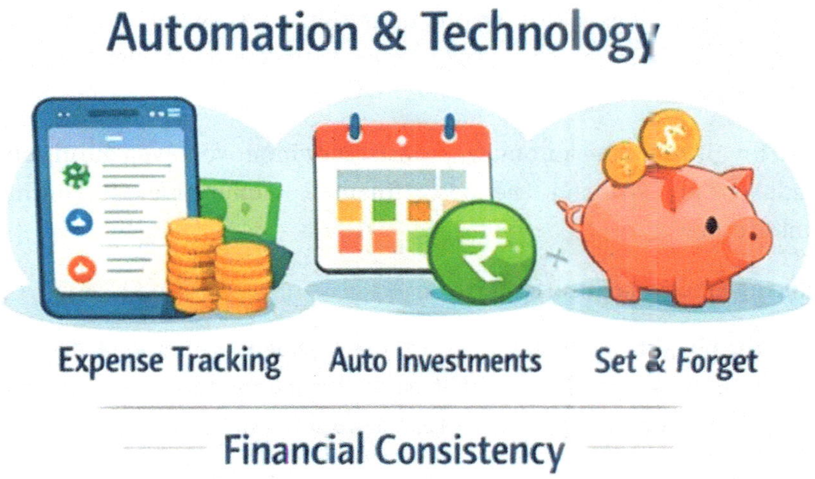

Digital Expense Tracking

Banking applications and expense-tracking platforms automatically categorize transactions into segments such as groceries, utilities, travel, and entertainment. This real-time visibility allows individuals to monitor spending patterns without manually recording every purchase. Over time, such tracking provides behavioural insights-highlighting areas of overspending or opportunities for optimization.

The benefit is awareness without effort. When data is organized automatically, decision-making becomes informed rather than emotional.

Automated Savings and Investments

Automation plays a crucial role in maintaining financial discipline. Systems such as:

- Monthly Systematic Investment Plans (SIPs)
- Scheduled transfers to emergency funds
- Recurring fixed deposits
- Automatic retirement contributions

ensure that savings occur before discretionary spending begins. This principle-often referred to as "pay yourself first"-strengthens long-term wealth creation.

When investments are automated, consistency improves. Even during busy schedules or stressful periods, financial commitments continue uninterrupted.

Reducing Emotional Interference

One of the biggest challenges in money management is emotional decision-making. Impulse spending, market panic during volatility, or postponing savings due to temporary pressures can disrupt financial progress.

Automation minimizes these behavioural risks. Since transfers and investments happen automatically, there is less opportunity to delay or avoid them. The system enforces discipline silently in the background.

Enhancing Long-Term Growth

Technology also enables portfolio tracking, performance dashboards, goal-based calculators, and alerts for bill payments. These tools create an integrated ecosystem where budgeting, saving, and investing are interconnected.

When systems operate consistently, financial growth becomes systematic rather than accidental. Over time, automation compounds both money and discipline.

Table: Role of Technology in Budget Management

Technology Tool	Primary Function	Benefit to User	Impact on Financial Discipline
Banking Apps	Real-time transaction tracking	Instant spending visibility	Improves awareness
Expense Trackers	Categorization and budgeting insights	Identifies spending patterns	Encourages informed decisions
Automated SIP Platforms	Scheduled monthly investments	Ensures consistent investing	Builds long-term wealth
Recurring Transfers	Auto-savings deposits	Prevents missed savings	Strengthens saving habit
Financial Dashboards	Goal tracking and performance review	Clear progress monitoring	Enhances motivation and control

4

Emergency Funds & Financial Safety Nets

4.1 Why Financial Resilience Matters More Than High Returns

Before chasing investment returns, financial stability must come first. An emergency fund acts as a buffer between unexpected events and long-term goals. Without it, even a minor financial shock-medical expense, job loss, urgent travel-can force withdrawal from investments or accumulation of debt.

In personal finance, many people focus first on maximizing returns-searching for the highest-yield investments, trending stocks, or aggressive growth strategies. However, strong returns are meaningful only when they are supported by financial stability. Without a secure foundation, even the best-performing portfolio can collapse under the pressure of unexpected life events. This is why financial resilience is more important than chasing high returns.

Financial resilience refers to the ability to withstand economic shocks without disrupting long-term financial goals. It is the protective layer that shields your financial plan from sudden disruptions such as medical emergencies, temporary unemployment, urgent travel, family obligations, or economic downturns. An emergency fund is the most practical example of this resilience. It functions as a safety net-typically covering three to six months of essential expenses-so that unexpected costs do not force you to sell investments at the wrong time or rely on high-interest debt.

When individuals invest aggressively without building this safety buffer, they expose themselves to unnecessary risk. For instance, if markets decline during a personal emergency, withdrawing funds can lock in losses and derail long-term compounding. Similarly, using credit cards or loans during crises can create debt burdens that outweigh any investment gains. In such cases, the pursuit of higher returns actually increases financial vulnerability.

Financial resilience is not rooted in fear or pessimism. Instead, it reflects strategic foresight. Markets are cyclical; economic slowdowns, inflationary periods, and volatility are natural parts of financial systems. On a personal level, income interruptions, health challenges, and life transitions are equally normal. A resilient financial structure acknowledges this uncertainty and prepares for it proactively.

Moreover, resilience strengthens decision-making. When individuals know they have a secure emergency fund, they can remain calm during market fluctuations. This emotional stability prevents impulsive actions such as panic selling or abandoning long-term investment plans. In this way, resilience indirectly supports better returns by promoting disciplined behaviour.

High returns may accelerate wealth creation, but resilience preserves it. Sustainable wealth-building is not a race to maximize gains at any cost; it is a structured process of balancing growth with protection. A solid financial foundation-emergency savings, manageable debt levels, insurance coverage, and diversified assets-creates the conditions necessary for investments to perform over time.

Ultimately, financial resilience ensures continuity. It allows you to stay invested, stay disciplined, and stay aligned with your goals, even when circumstances change. Growth without protection is fragile; growth supported by resilience is durable.

4.2 How Much Should You Save for Emergencies?

The size of an emergency fund depends on lifestyle, income stability, and dependents. A general guideline suggests maintaining three to six months of essential living expenses. Individuals with unstable income or business earnings may consider extending this to nine or even twelve months.

Essential expenses include housing, utilities, food, insurance premiums, and loan repayments. The focus is survival-level comfort-not luxury. Calculating this number gives clarity and transforms a vague goal into a measurable target.

An emergency fund is not a random savings amount-it should be calculated with intention. The right size depends on your personal circumstances, not a one-size-fits-all formula. Factors such as income stability, profession, family responsibilities, health conditions, and financial obligations all influence how much you should set aside.

A widely accepted guideline recommends maintaining **three to six months of essential living expenses**. This range works well for salaried individuals with relatively stable income and predictable monthly costs. However, if you are self-employed, run a business, work on commissions, or depend on irregular income streams, a larger cushion-**nine to twelve months of expenses**-may be more appropriate. Income volatility increases financial uncertainty, so a stronger buffer reduces stress and risk.

The key is understanding what qualifies as "essential expenses." These are the non-negotiable costs required to maintain basic living standards. They typically include:

- Rent or home loan payments
- Utility bills (electricity, water, gas, internet)
- Groceries and basic household supplies
- Insurance premiums (health, life, vehicle)
- Minimum loan repayments
- Transportation costs for work or daily needs

This calculation focuses on survival-level comfort-not lifestyle upgrades. Dining out, vacations, entertainment subscriptions, and discretionary shopping are excluded. The purpose of an emergency fund is to preserve stability, not to maintain luxury during temporary hardship.

For example, if your essential monthly expenses total ₹50,000, a six-month emergency fund would require ₹3,00,000. Seeing this number written down transforms a vague intention like "I should save more" into a concrete and measurable goal. Clarity makes planning realistic and achievable.

It is also wise to reassess your emergency fund periodically. Major life changes-marriage, having children, purchasing property, taking on new loans, or shifting careers-may increase your required reserve. As responsibilities grow, so should your financial cushion.

Ultimately, the purpose of an emergency fund is confidence. When you know that your basic needs are secured for several months, you gain the freedom to make rational financial decisions instead of reactive ones. Saving for emergencies is less about predicting disasters and more about building steady control over uncertainty.

Example 1: Salaried Employee with Stable Income

Profile:
Rahul works in a private company and earns ₹80,000 per month. His job is relatively stable.

Monthly Essential Expenses:

- Rent: ₹20,000
- Groceries: ₹8,000
- Utilities (electricity, water, internet): ₹5,000
- Insurance premiums: ₹4,000
- EMI (bike loan): ₹6,000
- Transport & fuel: ₹7,000

Total Essential Expenses = **₹50,000** per month

Since Rahul has stable income, he decides to keep 6 months of expenses.

₹50,000 × 6 = **₹3,00,000** emergency fund

This means if Rahul loses his job, he can survive for 6 months without touching his investments or taking loans.

Example 2: Self-Employed Business Owner

Profile:
Megha runs a small digital marketing agency. Her income fluctuates between ₹70,000 and ₹1,50,000 per month.

Monthly Essential Expenses:

- Home loan EMI: ₹30,000
- Groceries: ₹10,000
- Utilities: ₹6,000
- Insurance premiums: ₹5,000
- School fees (child): ₹8,000
- Basic household needs: ₹6,000

Total Essential Expenses = **₹65,000 per month**

Because her income is unpredictable and she has a dependent child, she chooses a 9-**month cushion**.

₹65,000 × 9 = **₹5,85,000** emergency fund

This gives her breathing space during slow business months.

Example 3: Young Professional Living with Parents

Profile:
Aman earns ₹45,000 per month and lives with his parents. He contributes partially to household expenses.

Essential Expenses:

- Contribution to home: ₹10,000
- Personal insurance: ₹3,000
- Transport: ₹5,000
- Basic personal expenses: ₹7,000

Total = **₹25,000 per month**

Since he has family support, he may start with **3 months of expenses**.

₹25,000 × 3 = **₹75,000 emergency fund**

4.3 Where to Park Your Emergency Fund

Safety and liquidity are the priorities for emergency savings. The objective is accessibility without exposure to high risk. Suitable options may include high-yield savings accounts, short-term fixed deposits, or liquid mutual funds depending on financial systems available in your region.
The key rule: emergency funds should not be invested in volatile assets like equities or long-term instruments where withdrawal may cause loss. Accessibility within 24–72 hours is ideal.

Once you calculate how much you need, the next important question is **where to keep it**. The purpose of an emergency fund is not growth-it is protection and accessibility. That changes the rules completely.

When choosing a parking option, two priorities must guide your decision:

1. **Capital Safety** – Your money should not fluctuate in value.
2. **Liquidity** – You should be able to access it quickly, ideally within 24–72 hours.

High returns are not the goal here. Stability is.

1. Savings Account (High-Liquidity Option)

A regular or high-interest savings account is the simplest and most accessible option. The money is available instantly through ATM, UPI, or online transfer.

Best for:

- Immediate access
- First layer of emergency fund

- Salaried individuals

Though the interest may be modest, the safety and speed of access make it ideal for short-notice emergencies like hospital admission or urgent travel.

2. Short-Term Fixed Deposits (Structured Safety)

Fixed deposits (FDs) with short tenures can offer slightly better returns while maintaining low risk. Some banks allow premature withdrawal with minimal penalty.

Best for:

- Second layer of emergency fund
- Funds not required instantly but within 1–3 days

Many people divide their emergency fund into smaller FDs so they can break only what is needed instead of the entire amount.

3. Liquid Mutual Funds (Low-Risk Market Option)

Liquid mutual funds invest in short-term debt instruments and typically allow redemption within one business day. While not completely risk-free, they are generally less volatile than equity investments.

Best for:

- Those comfortable with basic financial products
- Parking money while earning slightly better returns than savings accounts

However, even here, the objective is stability-not aggressive gains.

What to Avoid

Emergency funds should not be invested in:

- Equities or stock market instruments
- Long-term mutual funds

- Real estate
- Lock-in products like ELSS
- Retirement accounts

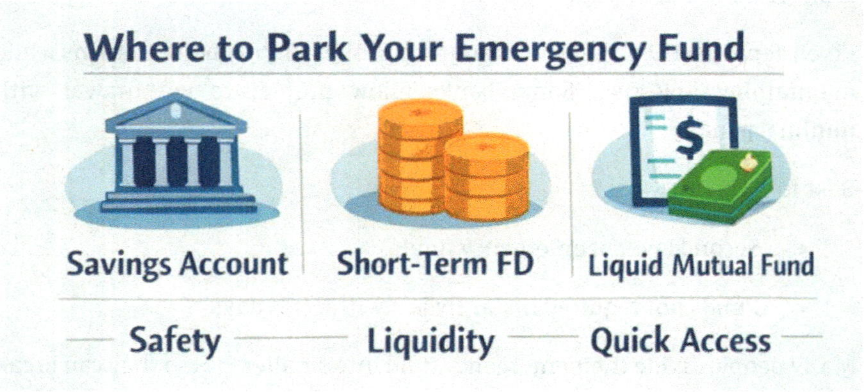

Why? Because market downturns or lock-in periods can prevent access or cause losses exactly when you need money most.

A Practical Structure

Many financially disciplined individuals follow a layered approach:

- 30–40% in savings account (instant access)
- 30–40% in short-term FD
- 20–30% in liquid fund

This balances accessibility with modest returns.

At its core, an emergency fund is not an investment-it is financial oxygen. You may never want to use it, but knowing it is available within 24–72 hours give you confidence and stability when life becomes unpredictable.

4.4 Beyond Savings: Insurance as a Financial Shield

An emergency fund handles short-term shocks, but insurance protects against large financial setbacks. Health insurance, term life insurance, and disability coverage reduce the risk of wealth destruction. Insurance should not be treated as an investment but as protection. Adequate coverage prevents a medical or accidental crisis from erasing years of savings. Together, emergency funds and insurance form a complete safety net.

An emergency fund is your first line of defence-but it has limits. It can cover temporary income gaps, urgent repairs, or short-term disruptions. However, large-scale financial shocks-major surgery, long-term hospitalization, permanent disability, or untimely death-can exceed even a well-built emergency reserve. This is where insurance becomes essential.

Insurance transfers financial risk from the individual to the insurer. Instead of bearing the full impact of a crisis yourself, you pay a predictable premium to protect against potentially devastating costs. It acts as a financial shock absorber for life's biggest uncertainties.

1. Health Insurance: Protecting Savings from Medical Inflation

Medical expenses can escalate quickly. A single hospitalization can consume several months-or even years-of savings. Health insurance ensures that your emergency fund remains intact for other needs while major medical costs are covered.

Key benefit:
It prevents a health crisis from becoming a financial crisis.

Without adequate coverage, people often liquidate investments or take high-interest loans during emergencies, which delays long-term wealth creation.

2. Term Life Insurance: Income Protection for Dependents

If you have dependents-spouse, children, aging parents-term life insurance becomes a responsibility rather than a choice. It provides a lump sum to your family in case of your untimely passing.

The goal is not investment growth but income replacement. Ideally, coverage should be sufficient to:

- Clear outstanding loans
- Cover children's education
- Support family living expenses for several years

This ensures that your financial plans continue even in your absence.

3. Disability Insurance: Safeguarding Earning Capacity

Your ability to earn is your greatest financial asset. A serious accident or long-term illness that reduces earning capacity can create prolonged financial strain. Disability coverage replaces a portion of income during such situations.

Many people underestimate this risk, focusing only on life coverage. But income interruption can be more financially damaging than many realize.

Insurance Is Protection, Not Investment

Insurance should never be purchased for returns. Policies that mix insurance and investment often dilute both objectives. Pure protection plans-like term insurance and health coverage-are generally more cost-effective and transparent.

The principle is simple:

- Emergency fund handles **manageable shocks** .
- Insurance protects against **catastrophic losses** .

Together, they form a complete financial safety net. One manages uncertainty; the other absorbs extreme risk. When both are in place, you build not just wealth-but stability that survives life's unpredictability.

Case Study: How Insurance Prevented Financial Collapse

Profile

Name: Arvind Sharma
Age: 35
Family: Wife and 1 child (age 5)
Monthly Income: ₹1,20,000
Monthly Essential Expenses: ₹70,000
Emergency Fund: ₹4,20,000 (6 months of expenses)

Arvind had done two things right:

- Built a 6-month emergency fund
- Purchased health insurance (₹10 lakh cover) and term life insurance (₹1 crore cover)

The Crisis

Arvind was diagnosed with a serious medical condition requiring hospitalization and surgery. Total medical cost: **₹8,50,000**.

He was also advised 3 months of rest, meaning temporary income disruption.

Scenario A: Without Insurance

If Arvind had no health insurance:

- Medical bills: ₹8,50,000
- Emergency fund available: ₹4,20,000
- Remaining gap: ₹4,30,000

He would have:

- Exhausted his entire emergency fund
- Liquidated investments or taken a loan
- Faced EMIs during recovery
- Delayed long-term goals like child education

One event would wipe out years of disciplined savings.

Scenario B: With Insurance

Because Arvind had a ₹10 lakh health policy:

- Insurance paid ₹8,20,000
- Arvind paid ₹30,000 (deductibles & minor expenses)

His emergency fund remained largely intact and was used only to manage household expenses during his 3-month recovery.

Result:

- No debt
- No forced withdrawal from investments
- No disruption to long-term financial goals

Key Learning

The emergency fund handled **short-term income loss** .
Insurance absorbed the **large medical expense** .

Together, they prevented financial destruction.

Bigger Insight

Many families believe savings alone are enough. But catastrophic expenses can exceed savings quickly. Insurance protects wealth from being erased, while savings provide liquidity.

Financial resilience is not built by choosing between savings and insurance. It is built by combining both strategically.

5

The Power of Compounding – Letting Time Work for You

5.1 Understanding Compounding in Simple Terms

Compounding is the process where earnings generate additional earnings over time. When interest or returns are reinvested, growth accelerates. Compounding is the quiet force that turns patience into power. It happens when the returns you earn on your investment begin to earn returns themselves. Instead of withdrawing interest or profits, you keep them invested. Over time, this creates a snowball effect-your money grows not just from what you originally invested, but also from the gains accumulated along the way.

Think of it like planting a tree. In the first year, it grows a few branches. In the next year, those branches grow new branches of their own. With each passing season, growth multiplies because it builds on what already exists. The same principle applies to money. If you invest ₹10,000 and earn returns, the next cycle's returns are calculated on ₹10,000 plus the earlier earnings. Those larger base keeps expanding.

The key factor in compounding is time. The longer your money stays invested, the more powerful the effect becomes. Even modest returns can grow into significant wealth when given enough years. This is why starting early matters more than investing large amounts later. A small investment made today often outperforms a bigger one made years down the line.

Consistency also plays a crucial role. Regular contributions strengthen the compounding process because each new addition begins generating its own returns. Over decades, this steady discipline can transform financial security from a goal into a reality.

In simple terms, compounding is money working for you-and then that money hiring more money to work as well.

5.2 The Cost of Delayed Investing

Many people postpone investing, believing they need large sums to begin. However, delay significantly reduces compounding potential. Starting early-even with small contributions-can result in greater wealth than starting later with higher amounts.
This demonstrates that time in the market is often more powerful than timing the market. Patience and consistency outperform sporadic investing.

Delaying investment may seem harmless, especially when someone feels they need a "bigger" amount to start. But the real cost of postponement is not just lost months or years-it is lost compounding. Every year you wait is a year your money could have been growing, multiplying, and building momentum.

Compounding rewards time more than size. When you start early, even modest contributions get the advantage of a longer growth runway. Over time, returns accumulate on top of returns, creating exponential growth. If you delay by five or ten years, you don't just lose those years of returns-you also lose the future returns those early gains would have generated. That opportunity rarely comes back.

Consider two investors: one begins at 25 with small monthly contributions, and another starts at 35 with double the amount. Surprisingly, the early starter may still end up with more wealth by retirement because their money had more time to compound. This clearly shows that duration often matters more than contribution size.

Another important lesson here is the difference between "time in the market" and "timing the market." Trying to predict perfect entry points can lead to missed opportunities and hesitation. Long-term consistency, on the other hand, allows investments to ride out short-term volatility and benefit from overall growth trends.

In essence, the biggest financial mistake is not starting small-it is not starting at all. Patience, discipline, and an early beginning can outperform occasional large investments made too late.

Illustration: Starting Early vs Starting Late

Assumptions:

- Annual return: 10%
- Investment period ends at age 60
- Monthly contribution as mentioned
- Compounding annually (simplified for clarity)

Scenario	Start Age	Monthly Investment	Years Invested	Total Invested (₹)	Approx. Final Value at 60 (₹)	Wealth Advantage
Early Starter	25	5,000	35	21,00,000	1,90,00,000+	Highest growth due to longer compounding
Late Starter	35	10,000	25	30,00,000	1,30,00,000+	Lower growth despite higher contribution

Key Insight

- The early investor contributed less total money yet accumulated significantly more wealth .

- The difference is not the contribution size-it is the **extra 10 years of compounding**.
- Time acts as a multiplier that cannot be replaced later with higher investment amounts.

5.3 Consistency Over Intensity

Wealth creation does not require aggressive or risky strategies. Instead, systematic and disciplined contributions build substantial portfolios. Monthly investments through systematic plans help smooth market fluctuations and reduce emotional decision-making.
Even modest contributions, if maintained over decades, can create significant financial outcomes. Consistency builds momentum, and momentum fuels compounding.

When it comes to building wealth, dramatic moves are often overrated. Many people assume that high returns require high risk or aggressive strategies. In reality, sustainable wealth is usually the result of steady, disciplined action rather than bursts of intensity.

Consistency means investing a fixed amount regularly-monthly or quarterly-regardless of market conditions. This approach reduces the temptation to react emotionally to market ups and downs. Instead of trying to predict the perfect moment to invest, you follow a systematic plan. Over time, this discipline smooths out market volatility because investments are made at different price levels. When prices are lower, you buy more units; when prices are higher, you buy fewer. This averaging effect reduces the impact of short-term fluctuations.

Another advantage of consistency is psychological stability. Sporadic investing often comes with stress-waiting for the "right time," fearing losses, or chasing sudden market rallies. A structured investment plan removes much of that emotional burden and encourages long-term thinking.

Most importantly, steady contributions build momentum. Each investment adds to the principal, and compounding begins working on an expanding base. Even modest monthly amounts can grow significantly when sustained over decades. The real strength lies not in how aggressively you invest, but in how reliably you continue.

In wealth creation, intensity may create excitement-but consistency creates results.

5.4 The Emotional Discipline Behind Long-Term Growth

Compounding rewards patience but tests emotions. Market downturns may tempt investors to withdraw funds prematurely. However, long-term investors understand that volatility is temporary while growth trends are long-term.
Emotional discipline-avoiding panic selling or impulsive switching-allows compounding to function effectively. Trusting the process and maintaining perspective ensures wealth accumulation continues uninterrupted.

Compounding sounds mathematical, but in practice, it is deeply psychological. The real challenge in long-term investing is not understanding returns-it is managing emotions. Markets naturally move in cycles. There will be phases of rapid growth and periods of decline. During downturns, fear becomes louder than logic, and many investors feel the urge to withdraw or switch strategies impulsively.

However, long-term wealth builders recognize an important distinction: volatility is temporary, but long-term economic growth has historically been upward. Short-term price movements often reflect uncertainty, news events, or sentiment-not permanent value destruction. Acting out of panic interrupts the compounding process, locking in losses and preventing recovery.

Emotional discipline means staying committed to a well-defined strategy even when headlines are negative. It requires resisting the temptation to time the market or chase quick gains elsewhere. Instead of reacting emotionally, disciplined investors review their goals, asset allocation, and time horizon before making decisions.

Perspective plays a crucial role. A one-year decline may feel significant, but when viewed across a 20- or 30-year investment horizon, it often becomes just a small fluctuation within a larger upward trend. Patience allows compounding to continue uninterrupted, and uninterrupted growth is what builds meaningful wealth.

Ultimately, long-term investing is less about predicting markets and more about controlling reactions. Trust in a structured plan, combined with emotional stability, allows compounding to perform its powerful work overtime.

Case Study: Emotional Discipline During a Market Crash

Background

Rahul, a 28-year-old salaried professional, began investing ₹15,000 per month through a systematic investment plan (SIP) in diversified equity mutual funds. His goal was long-term wealth creation for financial independence by age 55. He understood compounding and committed to staying invested for at least 25 years.

The Crisis

Three years into his investment journey, a major global market downturn occurred. Within six months, his portfolio value fell by nearly 30%. News headlines predicted prolonged recession. Many of Rahul's colleagues stopped their SIPs or redeemed investments to "protect what was left."

Rahul faced the same emotional pressure. Seeing his portfolio decline created anxiety and doubt. However, instead of reacting impulsively, he revisited his original plan:

- His investment horizon was still 25+ years.
- He had an emergency fund, so he did not need to withdraw money.
- Market downturns were historically temporary.

He decided to continue his SIP without interruption.

The Outcome

Over the next five years, markets gradually recovered and entered a strong growth phase. Because Rahul continued investing during the downturn, he accumulated more units at lower prices. When the market rebounded, those additional units significantly increased his portfolio value.

At the end of eight years:

Scenario	Action Taken	Portfolio Growth Impact
Panic Investor	Stopped SIP & withdrew during crash	Missed recovery gains; slower long-term growth
Disciplined Investor (Rahul)	Continued SIP consistently	Benefited from recovery; higher compounded returns

Rahul's portfolio not only recovered but surpassed previous highs. His disciplined approach accelerated compounding rather than interrupting it.

Key Lesson

Emotional discipline transforms volatility from a threat into an opportunity. Investors who maintain perspective during downturns allow compounding to continue working. The difference between long-term success and regret often lies not in market timing, but in emotional control.

6

Investing Basics – From Fear to Financial Confidence

6.1 Understanding Major Asset Classes

Investment options generally fall into categories such as equities (stocks), debt instruments (bonds or fixed-income securities), gold, and real estate.
Equities offer growth potential but carry volatility. Debt instruments provide stability and predictable returns. Gold often acts as a hedge during uncertainty. Real estate combines asset appreciation with possible rental income.
Diversifying across asset classes reduces overall risk and balances returns.

When individuals invest their money, they are essentially choosing *where their capital will work.* Most investment opportunities fall into four broad asset categories: equities, debt instruments, gold, and real estate. Each class behaves differently because it responds to economic conditions in its own way. Understanding these differences helps investors build balanced portfolios instead of relying on guesswork.

1. Equities (Stocks)

Equities represent ownership in a company. When you buy shares, you participate in the company's profits and growth. If the business expands, innovates, and increases earnings, the value of your shares may rise. Many companies also distribute part of their profits as dividends.

However, equities are sensitive to market sentiment, economic cycles, interest rates, and global events. Prices can fluctuate sharply in the short term. While they offer strong long-term growth potential, they require patience and the ability to tolerate volatility. Historically, equities have outperformed many other asset classes over extended periods, but they also involve higher risk.

2. Debt Instruments (Bonds and Fixed-Income Securities)

Debt instruments involve lending money to governments, corporations, or financial institutions in exchange for regular interest payments. Examples include government bonds, corporate bonds, and fixed deposits.

These investments are generally more stable than equities because they provide predictable income. The return is often fixed or relatively stable, making them suitable for conservative investors or those seeking income stability. However, returns from debt instruments are typically lower than long-term equity returns, and they can be affected by inflation and changes in interest rates.

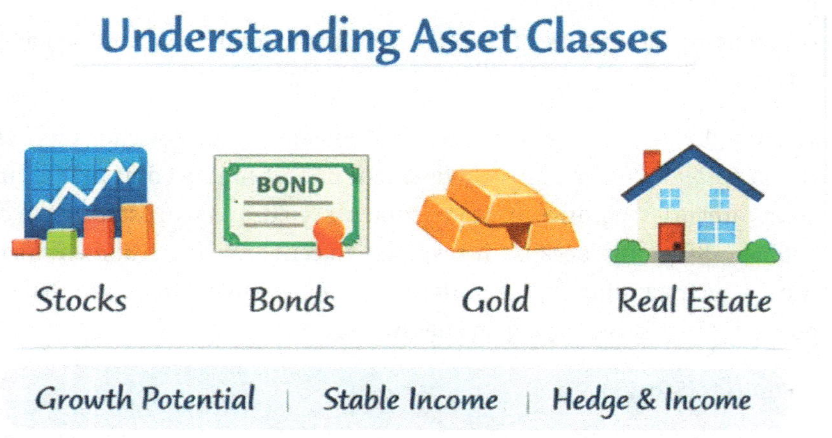

3. Gold

Gold is often viewed as a store of value rather than a productive asset. It does not generate income like dividends or interest. Instead, investors buy gold to preserve purchasing power or protect wealth during economic instability.

During periods of inflation, currency weakness, or geopolitical uncertainty, gold prices often rise as investors seek safety. This makes gold a useful hedge in a diversified portfolio. However, since it does not produce regular cash flow, it should usually complement other growth-oriented assets rather than replace them.

4. Real Estate

Real estate includes residential, commercial, or industrial property. It offers two potential benefits: capital appreciation (increase in property value) and rental income. Property values tend to grow over time in expanding economies, particularly in urban areas.

However, real estate requires substantial capital, involves maintenance costs, and may lack liquidity compared to stocks or bonds. Selling property takes time and transaction costs can be high. Despite this, it remains a popular long-term wealth-building asset.

The Importance of Diversification

Each asset class reacts differently to economic conditions. When stock markets decline, bonds may remain stable. When inflation rises, gold may perform well. Real estate may benefit from urban growth trends.

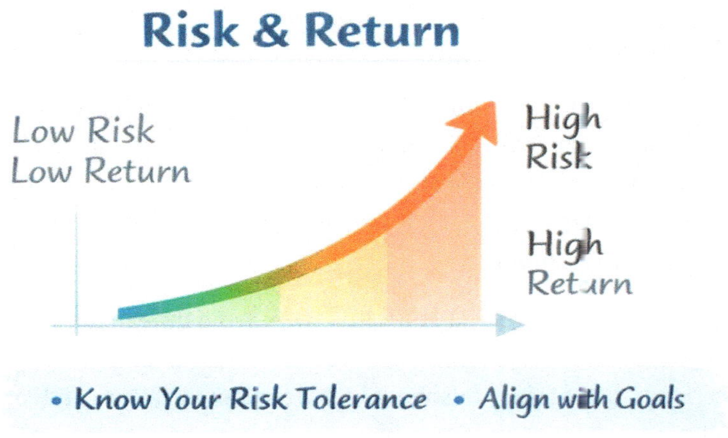

By spreading investments across different asset classes, investors reduce overall risk. Losses in one category can be offset by stability or gains in another. This strategic allocation helps balance growth and security, making the portfolio more resilient over time.

In essence, understanding asset classes is not about choosing one "best" option - it is about combining them intelligently to align with financial goals, risk tolerance, and time horizon.

6.2 Risk and Return: Finding Your Comfort Zone

Every investment carries some level of risk. Higher potential returns usually come with higher volatility. Understanding personal risk tolerance is essential before investing.
Young investors with stable income may tolerate higher equity exposure. Those nearing retirement may prioritize capital preservation. Aligning risk with financial goals prevents anxiety-driven decisions.

Every investment involves uncertainty. Risk, in financial terms, refers to the possibility that actual returns may differ from expected returns - including the chance of losing part of your capital. Return, on the other hand, is the reward you earn for taking that risk. The relationship between risk and return is fundamental: investments offering higher potential returns generally experience greater price fluctuations.

The Risk–Return Trade-Off

Equities, for example, can deliver strong long-term growth but often fluctuate significantly in the short term. Debt instruments provide more predictable income but typically offer lower returns. The key is recognizing that higher return potential comes with higher volatility - and volatility can test emotional discipline.

Understanding this trade-off helps investors avoid unrealistic expectations. If someone desires double-digit returns but panics during market corrections, there is a mismatch between expectation and emotional capacity.

Understanding Risk Tolerance

Risk tolerance is deeply personal. It reflects how much uncertainty an individual can handle without losing confidence or making impulsive decisions. It is influenced by:

- Age
- Income stability
- Financial responsibilities
- Investment knowledge
- Emotional temperament

Two people with identical incomes may respond very differently to market swings. One may stay calm during a 20% drop; another may sell in fear. Recognizing this difference is critical.

Life Stage and Asset Allocation

Investment strategy should evolve with life stages.

- **Young investors with steady income** often have time on their side. They can tolerate temporary market downturns because they have years - even decades - to recover. A higher allocation to equities may be suitable for long-term wealth creation.

- **Individuals approaching retirement** typically prioritize protecting accumulated wealth. Since they may soon depend on their savings for income, preserving capital becomes more important than aggressive growth. A greater allocation toward stable, income-generating assets often makes sense.

Aligning Risk with Financial Goals

Investments should match clearly defined goals. Short-term objectives, such as buying a home within three years, require lower risk exposure. Long-term goals like retirement planning may allow for more growth-oriented investments.

When risk levels are aligned with financial objectives and personal comfort, investors are less likely to make anxiety-driven decisions during market volatility. Emotional stability is just as important as financial strategy.

In the end, successful investing is not about chasing the highest return. It is about finding the level of risk that allows you to stay consistent, disciplined, and confident through market cycles.

6.3 Diversification: The Principle of Balance

Diversification spreads investments across industries, asset classes, and geographies. This reduces dependence on a single performance driver. If one sector underperforms, others may compensate. Diversification does not eliminate risk entirely but mitigates concentration risk. Balanced portfolios tend to experience smoother long-term growth.

Diversification is the practice of spreading investments across different categories so that your financial future does not depend on a single outcome. Instead of putting all capital into one company, one sector, or one country, investors distribute funds strategically. The goal is simple: reduce vulnerability to any one source of risk.

Spreading Across Asset Classes

A diversified portfolio typically includes a mix of asset classes such as equities, fixed income, gold, and real estate. Each asset class reacts differently to economic events. For example, when stock markets face volatility, bonds may remain relatively stable. During inflationary periods, gold may perform better.

By combining assets that behave differently under similar conditions, investors reduce the likelihood of extreme portfolio swings. This approach strengthens financial resilience over time.

Diversifying Across Industries

Even within equities, concentration risk can be significant. Investing heavily in one sector - such as technology, banking, or energy - exposes an investor to sector-specific risks. Regulatory changes, technological disruption, or commodity price shifts can severely affect a single industry.

Spreading investments across multiple industries reduces the impact of sector-specific downturns. If one industry underperforms, gains in another may offset the decline.

Geographic Diversification

Economic growth does not occur uniformly across the world. Some countries expand rapidly while others experience slowdowns. Political events, currency fluctuations, and trade policies can influence regional markets differently.

By investing across domestic and international markets, investors reduce dependence on one economy. Geographic diversification adds another layer of stability to long-term wealth building.

The Reality of Risk Management

Diversification does not eliminate risk. Market-wide events can affect multiple asset classes simultaneously. However, it significantly reduces concentration risk - the danger of large losses due to overexposure to a single investment theme.

Balanced portfolios often show smoother performance over long periods. They may not deliver the highest returns during market booms, but they also tend to cushion losses during downturns. This steadier trajectory helps investors remain disciplined and avoid emotional decision-making.

In essence, diversification is not about chasing maximum gains. It is about creating a structure that allows consistent growth while protecting against avoidable shocks. Balance, not prediction, is the real strategy behind long-term financial success.

Diversification Type	What It Means	Example	Key Benefit	Risk Reduced
Asset Class Diversification	Investing across different asset categories	Stocks + Bonds + Gold + Real Estate	Balances growth and stability	Market volatility risk
Industry Diversification	Spreading investments across sectors	IT + Pharma + Banking + FMCG	Reduces sector-specific exposure	Sector concentration risk
Geographic Diversification	Investing across different countries/regions	India + US + Europe + Emerging Markets	Protects against local slowdowns	Country-specific economic risk

6.4 Building an Investment Plan with Clarity

An investment plan should define objectives, time horizon, asset allocation, and review frequency. Goal-based investing-such as planning for retirement, children's education, or property purchase-gives direction.

Regular portfolio reviews ensure alignment with changing life circumstances. Adjustments should be strategic, not reactive. A structured investment plan transforms uncertainty into confidence and turns money into a productive asset.

An investment plan is not a list of products. It is a structured roadmap that connects money to meaningful life goals. Without a plan investing often becomes reactive - driven by trends, fear, or short-term market noise. With clarity, it becomes purposeful and disciplined.

1. Defining Clear Objectives

Every strong investment plan begins with defining specific financial goals. These goals may include retirement planning, funding children's education, purchasing property, building an emergency corpus, or achieving financial independence.

Clear goals answer essential questions:

- What is the target amount?
- When is it needed?
- How much risk can be taken to achieve it?

Goal-based investing provides direction. Instead of asking, "Which stock should I buy?," the question becomes, "What allocation strategy helps me reach this goal within this timeline?"

2. Determining Time Horizon

Time horizon plays a critical role in investment decisions. Short-term goals (1–3 years) require capital protection and lower volatility. Medium-term goals (3–7 years) may allow balanced exposure. Long-term goals (10+ years) can accommodate higher growth-oriented assets.

The longer the time horizon, the greater the capacity to absorb temporary market fluctuations. Time reduces the impact of short-term volatility and allows compounding to work effectively.

3. Strategic Asset Allocation

Asset allocation refers to the distribution of investments across different asset classes such as equities, debt, gold, and real estate. Research consistently shows that asset allocation contributes significantly to long-term portfolio performance.

Allocation should reflect:

- Risk tolerance
- Financial responsibilities
- Income stability
- Life stage

A young professional may allocate more toward equities for growth, while someone nearing retirement may emphasize income-generating assets. The key is balance aligned with personal circumstances.

4. Regular Review and Rebalancing

Life changes. Income grows, responsibilities increase, priorities shift. Therefore, an investment plan should not remain static. Periodic reviews - annually or semi-annually - help ensure that the portfolio remains aligned with goals.

Rebalancing involves restoring the original asset allocation when market movements distort proportions. For example, if equities grow significantly and exceed their intended percentage, some profits may be shifted to debt instruments to maintain balance.

The important distinction: adjustments should be strategic, not emotional. Reacting to short-term market panic often leads to poor decisions. Planned reviews promote discipline and confidence.

The Power of Structure

A structured investment plan transforms uncertainty into clarity. Instead of worrying about daily market movements, investors focus on progress toward defined goals.

When money is assigned a purpose, it becomes a productive asset rather than idle savings. Discipline replaces anxiety. Strategy replaces speculation. Over time, this structured approach builds not only wealth but also stability and peace of mind.

Summary Table: Key Components of an Investment Plan

Component	Purpose	Key Questions to Answer
Financial Objectives	Define what you are investing for	What amount? By when? For which goal?
Time Horizon	Determines risk capacity	Short-term or long-term?
Asset Allocation	Balances growth and stability	What % in equity, debt, gold, real estate?
Review Frequency	Maintains alignment with goals	How often will the portfolio be reviewed?
Rebalancing Strategy	Controls risk drift	When and how will allocation be corrected?

7

Multiple Streams of Income – Making Money Multiply

7.1 Why Relying on One Income Source Is Risky

Depending solely on a salary creates financial vulnerability. If employment stops, income stops. Economic downturns, company restructuring, health issues, or technological disruption can suddenly affect earning capacity.
Diversifying income streams reduces dependency risk. Just as investment portfolios benefit from diversification, personal income sources also gain stability through variety.
Building your entire financial life around a single paycheck may feel stable-until it isn't. A salary can create a sense of security because it arrives regularly and predictably. However, when income depends entirely on one employer, your financial well-being becomes tightly linked to factors beyond your control. Organizational restructuring, layoffs, automation, economic recessions, industry decline, or even personal health challenges can abruptly interrupt earnings. When that one source stops, the financial impact is immediate and often severe.

Modern economies are increasingly dynamic. Technological advancements, artificial intelligence, outsourcing, and global competition are reshaping job markets at a rapid pace. Roles that seem secure today may evolve or disappear tomorrow. Relying solely on employment income in such an environment increases vulnerability because it offers no built-in backup plan.

Diversifying income sources functions much like diversifying investments. In finance, investors reduce risk by spreading capital across different assets rather than placing everything into one stock. Similarly, individuals can strengthen financial stability by cultivating multiple streams of income. These may include rental property earnings, dividend income from investments, consulting or freelance projects, online businesses, royalties, or part-time ventures aligned with personal skills.

Multiple income streams provide three major advantages:

1. **Risk Reduction** – If one stream declines or stops, others can continue generating cash flow.
2. **Income Stability** – Combined streams often smooth out fluctuations in earnings.
3. **Growth Potential** – Additional income sources can accelerate wealth accumulation beyond the limits of a salary increase.

For example, during economic slowdowns, individuals who supplement their salaries with rental income or dividend-paying investments often face less financial strain. Even if their primary job income decreases, passive or semi-passive earnings help cover essential expenses.

Aspect	Single Income Source (Salary Only)	Multiple Income Sources (Diversified)
Income Stability	Fully dependent on employer continuity	Income continues even if one stream stops
Risk Exposure	High – job loss immediately stops earnings	Lower – other streams cushion financial shock
Control Level	Limited control over salary growth	Greater control through self-managed streams
Economic Downturn Impact	Severe impact if layoffs occur	Reduced stress due to alternative cash flows
Wealth Creation Speed	Slow – dependent on increments and promotions	Faster – parallel income growth possible
Financial Resilience	Weak during emergencies	Stronger due to diversified cash inflow
Flexibility	Restricted by employment terms	Flexible income timing and structure
Retirement Readiness	Relies on savings from one stream	Passive income supports long-term security
Psychological Security	Anxiety during job uncertainty	Confidence due to income backup options

Importantly, diversification does not require immediate large investments. It can begin gradually-such as monetizing a skill, building a digital product, or investing systematically in income-generating assets. Over time, these streams compound, increasing both financial resilience and long-term independence.

In essence, depending on one income source concentrates risk, while diversifying income distributes it. Financial security in today's unpredictable environment is less about earning more from one source and more about earning from multiple, strategically aligned sources.

7.2 Active vs. Passive Income: Understanding the Difference

Active income requires continuous effort-such as salaries, consulting, or freelance services. Passive income generates earnings with minimal ongoing involvement after initial setup.

When we talk about income, the real distinction isn't just how much you earn-it's **how your time is connected to that earning** .

Active income is directly tied to your effort and hours worked. If you stop working, the income stops. Salaries, consulting fees, freelance services, commissions, and hourly wages all fall into this category. Active income provides structure and predictability, but it depends heavily on your physical presence, time, and energy.

On the other hand, **passive income** is designed to generate money even when you are not actively working every day. It often requires significant upfront effort-such as investment, content creation, or system building-but once established, it continues producing earnings with limited ongoing involvement.

Passive income does not mean "zero effort." It means **front-loaded effort followed by recurring returns** .

Examples of Passive Income:

- Dividend-paying stocks
- Rental property income
- Digital products such as e-books or online courses
- Royalty-based creative work (books, music, patents)
- Automated online businesses

The key difference lies in scalability. Active income grows linearly-you earn more by working more. Passive income can grow exponentially-after setup, earnings may continue without proportionally increasing effort.

Case Illustration

Consider a full-time professional who creates an online course based on their expertise. Initially, they invest time in content creation, recording, editing, and marketing. During this phase, it feels like active effort. However, once the course is launched and automated sales systems are in place, it begins generating recurring revenue without daily involvement.

While they continue their full-time job (active income), the course becomes a parallel passive income stream. Over time, this additional earnings source can fund investments, accelerate savings goals, and reduce financial dependency on a single paycheck.

Financial independence is rarely built on active income alone. The strategic combination of active and passive streams creates both stability and long-term growth potential.

Table: Active vs. Passive Income Comparison

Parameter	Active Income	Passive Income
Effort Requirement	Continuous effort required	Initial effort, limited ongoing effort
Time Dependency	Directly linked to hours worked	Not directly tied to daily work hours
Income Flow	Stops if work stops	Continues even when not actively working
Scalability	Limited by personal capacity	Potentially scalable beyond time limits
Risk Level	Stable but dependent on employer/clients	May fluctuate depending on asset performance
Examples	Salary, consulting, freelancing	Dividends, rental income, digital products

Wealth Building Potential	Gradual growth	Compounding and long-term growth

7.3 Building Scalable Income Systems

Scalability refers to the ability to increase earnings without proportional increases in effort. Traditional employment often lacks scalability because income rises slowly.
Digital platforms, investments, and business ownership offer scalability.

If income is tied strictly to your time, growth will always be limited. There are only 24 hours in a day. Scalability changes that equation.

Scalability means increasing earnings without increasing effort at the same rate. In simple terms, your income grows faster than your workload. Traditional employment models are usually linear-you work more, you earn slightly more. Promotions and increments happen gradually, often capped by organizational structure.

Scalable systems, however, are built on leverage.

Leverage can come from:

- **Technology** (digital platforms, automation)
- **Capital** (investments that compound)
- **Systems** (repeatable processes)
- **Ownership** (equity in businesses or assets)

When you create or invest in scalable systems, your income becomes less dependent on personal labour and more dependent on structure.

1. Investment-Based Scalability

Dividend-paying stocks are a classic example. Initially, a modest investment may produce small quarterly payouts. But when those dividends are reinvested, they purchase additional shares. Over time, this creates a compounding cycle-more shares generate more dividends, which generate even more shares.

Eventually, dividend income may grow enough to cover essential monthly expenses. The effort required does not increase proportionally, but the income does.

That is scalability through capital.

2. Digital Scalability

Digital products are another powerful example. An e-book, online course, or software tool requires upfront effort. But once created, it can be sold to hundreds or thousands of customers worldwide without recreating the product each time.

An e-commerce product listed on a global marketplace can reach customers across cities, countries, or continents. Operational systems-such as automated payments, fulfilment partners, and digital marketing-allow growth without direct daily involvement for every sale.

That is scalability through technology.

3. Business Ownership Scalability

Owning a business allows income to grow through team expansion, operational optimization, and market reach. Instead of exchanging time for money, you build systems where processes generate revenue.

Employees, automation, and distribution channels act as multipliers.

Key Characteristics of Scalable Income Systems

Factor	Non-Scalable Income (Traditional Salary)	Scalable Income System
Growth Pattern	Linear	Exponential or compound-based
Effort Required	Increases with income	Does not increase proportionally

Dependency	Dependent on personal time	Dependent on systems/assets
Geographic Reach	Limited to workplace	Global through digital platforms
Wealth Acceleration	Slow	Potentially rapid over time
Long-Term Potential	Capped by role	Limited by strategy and execution

Why Scalable Systems Matter

In an uncertain economic environment, scalable income systems create:

- Financial resilience
- Faster wealth accumulation
- Reduced dependency on a single employer
- Long-term passive cash flow

The goal is not to abandon active income immediately. Instead, it is to gradually build scalable systems alongside primary employment. Over time, these systems shift your financial structure from effort-driven income to asset-driven income.

That transition is where financial independence truly begins.

7.4 Managing Multiple Income Streams Strategically

Diversifying income does not mean chasing every opportunity. Each stream should align with personal skills, available time, and financial goals.

It is essential to:

- Maintain proper financial records
- Allocate income wisely between reinvestment and lifestyle
- Avoid burnout by overextending

Let's be honest-diversifying income sounds exciting. But here's the truth: more income streams don't automatically mean more success . If managed poorly, they can create stress, confusion, and burnout.

Strategic diversification is not about chasing every trend or opportunity. It's about building income sources that align with:

- Your existing skills
- Your available time
- Your risk tolerance
- Your long-term financial goals

Without alignment, multiple streams can become multiple distractions.

1. Alignment Before Expansion

Before starting a new income stream, ask:

- Does this leverage my strengths?
- Can I manage it without compromising my primary responsibilities?
- Does it support my long-term wealth plan?

For example, a finance professional might find dividend investing more aligned than launching a restaurant. A teacher might scale through online courses rather than speculative trading.

Strategic choices reduce unnecessary risk.

2. Maintain Clear Financial Records

When income streams multiply, financial complexity increases. Proper bookkeeping becomes essential. Separate accounts, structured expense tracking, tax planning, and performance analysis help ensure each stream remains profitable.

Without tracking:

- You may overestimate profits.
- You may underestimate costs.

- Tax liabilities can become burdensome.

Clarity prevents chaos.

3. Balance Reinvestment and Lifestyle

New income often creates temptation to increase lifestyle spending immediately. However, strategic wealth builders allocate income carefully:

- A portion for reinvestment (to grow the stream)
- A portion for savings and investments
- A portion for lifestyle upgrades

Reinvestment fuels compounding. Lifestyle inflation slows it.

4. Avoid Burnout Through Structured Scaling

One of the biggest risks in managing multiple streams is overextension. Working full-time while running side businesses, managing investments, and handling personal responsibilities can quickly become overwhelming.

Smart scaling means:

- Automating where possible
- Delegating tasks
- Growing gradually instead of aggressively

Growth should increase freedom-not eliminate it.

Case Study: Gradual Rental Portfolio Growth

Consider an individual with a stable full-time job who aims to build rental income. Instead of acquiring several properties quickly using high debt, they purchase one property at a time over ten years.

Each property is:

- Carefully evaluated

- Financed conservatively
- Supported by stable cash flow

As rental income grows, it begins covering major household expenses-such as loan EMIs, utilities, or school fees. Over time, dependence on salary decreases.

Because the expansion was gradual and financially disciplined:

- Risk remained controlled
- Debt remained manageable
- Financial stress stayed low

The result? A sustainable, stress-free secondary income stream that strengthens overall financial stability.

Table: Strategic vs. Unstructured Income Diversification

Factor	Unstructured Diversification	Strategic Diversification
Decision Basis	Trends and excitement	Skills and long-term goals
Financial Tracking	Irregular or unclear	Structured and documented
Debt Usage	Aggressive leverage	Controlled and planned
Stress Level	High	Managed
Growth Pace	Rapid but unstable	Gradual and sustainable
Long-Term Outcome	Burnout or financial strain	Stability and resilience

Managing multiple income streams is less about quantity and more about quality. When structured properly, diversified income reduces risk, accelerates wealth building, and enhances financial confidence-without sacrificing balance.

8

Smart Tax Planning & Wealth Protection

8.1 Understanding the Impact of Taxes on Wealth

Taxes significantly influence long-term returns. Even modest tax inefficiencies can reduce investment growth over decades. Effective tax planning involves using legitimate deductions, exemptions, and tax-efficient instruments to retain more of your earnings.

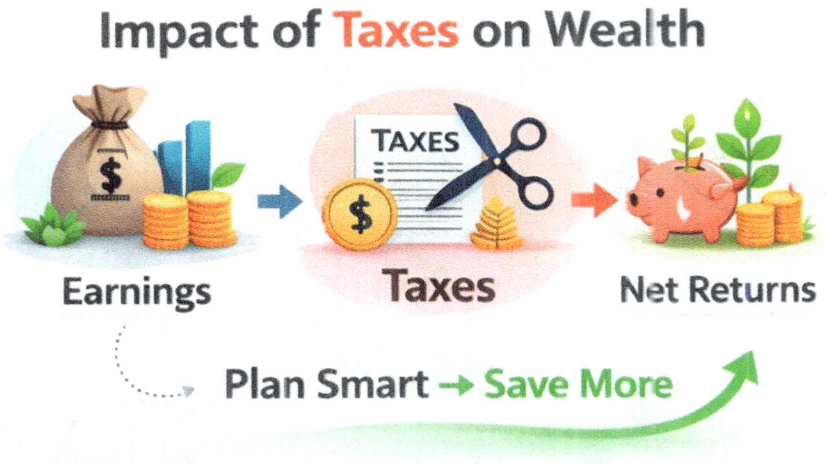

Taxes are one of the most underestimated factors affecting long-term wealth creation. While investors often focus on interest rates, market returns, and risk levels, the portion of earnings lost to taxation can quietly shape the final outcome of an investment journey. Over time, even small differences in tax treatment can create a noticeable gap in accumulated wealth.

When you earn returns-whether through salary, interest, dividends, rental income, or capital gains-a percentage is typically paid to the government. If investments are structured without considering taxation, a portion of gains is consistently reduced before it can compound further. Compounding works best when returns remain invested and continue to grow. However, when taxes are deducted frequently or at higher rates, the compounding effect weakens because less capital stays invested to generate future returns.

This is why tax planning is not about avoiding taxes but about organizing finances intelligently within legal frameworks. Effective tax planning means selecting investment options that offer deductions, exemptions, deferment benefits, or lower tax rates on gains. For example, certain long-term investments may be taxed more favourably than short-term trades. Some financial instruments may provide tax deductions on contributions, while others may offer tax-free withdrawals at maturity. Choosing the right mix can significantly improve net returns.

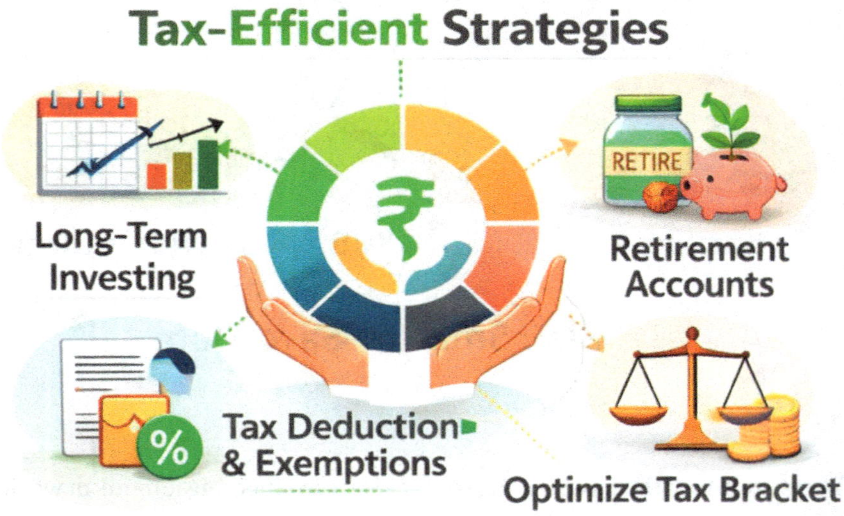

Consider two investors who both earn an annual return of 10% over 20 years. The first investor pays higher taxes each year due to frequent trading or choosing fully taxable instruments. The second investor uses tax-efficient options and benefits from lower capital gains taxes or deferred taxation. Although their gross returns are identical, the second investor retains a larger portion of earnings annually. Over two decades this difference compounds, resulting in a substantially larger final portfolio value.

Taxes, therefore, should be treated as a strategic element of wealth management. Thoughtful planning ensures that more of what you earn remains invested, accelerating long-term financial growth while staying fully compliant with the law.

8.2 Tax-Efficient Investment Strategies

Different financial instruments are taxed differently. Some offer benefits for long-term holding, retirement savings, or insurance-linked investment.
Strategies may include:

- Long-term investing to reduce capital gains tax
- Utilizing retirement accounts
- Structuring investments for optimal tax brackets

Illustration:
An investor shifts short-term speculative trading to long-term diversified investing. Over years, reduced transaction frequency and favourable tax treatment increase net returns.

Not all investments are taxed in the same way-and that difference can quietly shape your long-term wealth. Interest income, dividends, short-term gains, and long-term capital gains often fall under different tax rules. When investors ignore this, they may unknowingly reduce their effective return. Smart investors, however, align their investment choices with tax efficiency to protect and grow their capital.

One powerful strategy is **long-term investing** . In many tax systems, gains from assets held for a longer duration are taxed at a lower rate than short-term profits. Frequent buying and selling not only increases transaction costs but may also trigger higher taxes. By staying invested in quality assets over time, investors allow compounding to work uninterrupted while benefiting from favourable long-term capital gains treatment.

Another approach is **utilizing retirement-focused accounts or tax-advantaged schemes** . These accounts often provide deductions at the time of contribution, tax-deferred growth, or reduced tax upon withdrawal. The advantage here is timing-money that would otherwise go toward taxes remains invested and compounds for years before any tax liability arises.

A third strategy involves **structuring investments to manage tax brackets** . For instance, spreading withdrawals across years, balancing taxable and tax-free instruments, or aligning investments with income levels can help prevent unnecessary movement into higher tax brackets. Proper structuring ensures that taxes are optimized without taking excessive risk.

Consider an investor who once engaged in frequent short-term trades. High turnover led to higher taxes and brokerage costs. After shifting to a diversified, long-term portfolio, trading frequency declined, taxes on gains reduced, and compounding strengthened. Over several years, the investor noticed higher net returns-even though average annual market performance remained similar.

Tax-efficient investing is not about chasing loopholes; it is about making thoughtful, compliant decisions that allow more of your returns to stay invested. Over time, this disciplined approach can significantly improve overall wealth accumulation.

8.3 Insurance as a Wealth Preservation Tool

Wealth creation without protection is incomplete. Health emergencies, accidents, or premature death can reverse financial progress. Essential protective tools include:

- Health insurance
- Term life insurance
- Disability coverage

Insurance prevents forced liquidation of investments during crises.

Building wealth is important - but protecting it is equally critical. Many people focus heavily on investing and growing their assets yet overlook the risks that can suddenly disrupt financial stability. Unexpected health issues, accidents, disabilities, or the premature loss of an earning member can derail years of disciplined savings if proper protection is not in place. Wealth creation without protection is like constructing a building without a foundation.

Insurance acts as a financial safety net. It does not create wealth directly, but it protects the wealth you are working hard to build.

Health insurance safeguards savings from medical expenses.
Hospitalization, surgeries, or long-term treatments can be extremely expensive. Without coverage, families often dip into emergency funds, break fixed deposits, or sell investments to meet costs.

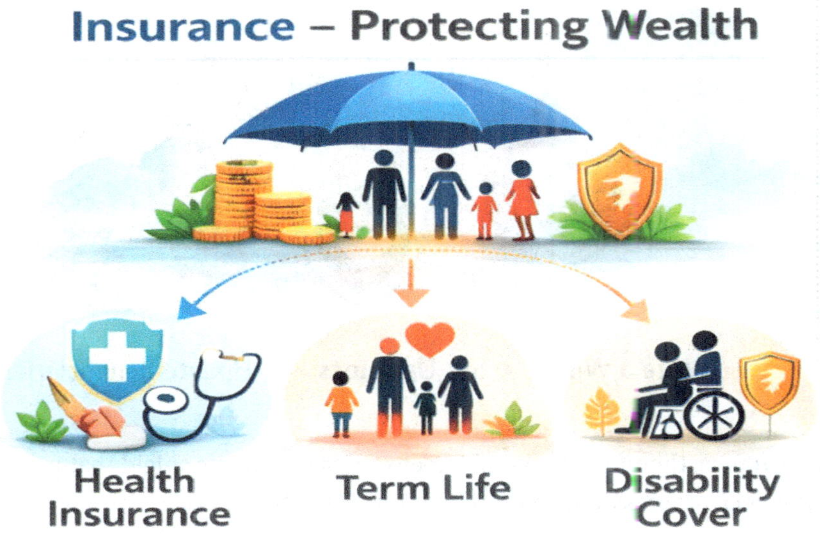

Term life insurance ensures financial continuity for dependents in the event of an untimely death. It replaces income and helps cover essential obligations such as loans, education expenses, or household needs. Unlike investment-linked insurance, pure term plans provide higher coverage at relatively lower cost, making them efficient protection tools.

Disability coverage is often ignored but equally important. A disability can reduce earning capacity for years, affecting long-term financial plans. This insurance protects income when the ability to work is compromised.

Consider two families. The first lacks adequate insurance and faces a major medical emergency. To pay hospital bills, they sell long-term investments during a market downturn, locking in losses and disrupting future compounding. The second family, protected by health coverage, manages expenses through insurance claims and keeps their investment portfolio intact. Over time, the protected family continues to benefit from growth, while the other struggles to rebuild.

Insurance, therefore, is not an expense-it is a strategic shield that preserves financial progress and ensures long-term stability.

8.4 Estate Planning and Asset Transfer

Wealth protection extends beyond one's lifetime. Estate planning ensures assets are distributed according to personal wishes while

minimizing legal complications.
Key components include:

- Writing a clear will
- Nomination in financial accounts
- Trust structures for dependents

Planning ahead reduces disputes and preserves financial continuity for future generations.

Wealth management does not end with accumulation and protection during one's lifetime. A complete financial plan also considers what happens to assets after death. Estate planning ensures that wealth is transferred smoothly, legally, and according to personal intentions. Without clear planning, families may face delays, disputes, emotional strain, and unnecessary legal expenses.

One of the most fundamental elements of estate planning is **writing a clear and legally valid will**. A will specifies how assets-such as property, investments, business interests, or personal valuables-should be distributed. It also allows individuals to appoint guardians for minor children and name executors responsible for carrying out instructions. Without a will, assets are distributed according to default succession laws, which may not reflect personal wishes.

Another essential step is **updating nominations in financial accounts**. Bank accounts, insurance policies, retirement funds, and investment portfolios typically allow nomination of beneficiaries. Proper nomination ensures quicker access to funds for family members and reduces administrative delays. However, nominations should align with the broader estate plan to avoid inconsistencies.

For more complex family situations, **trust structures** can provide added protection. Trusts are especially useful when there are minor children, dependents with special needs, or family business assets that require structured management. They help control how and when assets are distributed while protecting beneficiaries from mismanagement or external claims.

Planning in advance preserves financial continuity. It reduces conflict, ensures clarity, and protects loved ones from uncertainty during emotionally difficult times. Estate planning is not only about transferring assets-it is about transferring stability, intention, and long-term security across generations.

Case Study: The Importance of Estate Planning in Asset Transfer

Mr. Sharma, a successful entrepreneur, accumulated significant wealth over three decades. His assets included residential property, commercial real estate, equity investments, fixed deposits, and a family business. Confident that his family "understood his intentions," he never formally prepared a will or structured his estate plan.

After his sudden demise, complications began to surface. Although his wife and two children had a close relationship, disagreements arose regarding ownership of the business and distribution of properties. Some bank accounts had outdated nominations, and certain investments had no nominees at all. As a result, portions of the estate became subject to lengthy legal procedures. The business operations slowed due to uncertainty in leadership, and legal costs reduced the overall value of the estate. Emotional strain further affected family harmony.

In contrast, consider Mrs. Mehta, who had a comparable asset base. She prepared a legally valid will, updated nominations across all financial accounts, and created a trust for her minor granddaughter's education. She clearly documented how the family business would transition to her son while allocating investment assets equitably among heirs.

Upon her passing, the estate transfer process was orderly and transparent. Financial institutions processed claims quickly due to proper nominations. The trust ensured uninterrupted funding for education expenses. Because her intentions were clearly documented, disputes were avoided and the family business continued smoothly.

The difference between the two families highlights a crucial lesson: estate planning is not only about distributing wealth, but about preserving stability, clarity, and unity for future generations.

9

Financial Freedom Blueprint – Designing Your Exit Strategy

9.1 Defining Financial Freedom on Your Terms

Financial freedom is not about extreme wealth; it is about choice. It means having enough income-generating assets to cover essential living expenses without active employment.
Each individual's freedom definition differs. Some seek early retirement; others seek flexibility to pursue passion projects.

Financial freedom is often misunderstood as becoming extremely wealthy. In reality, it is far more personal and practical. Financial freedom means having the ability to make life decisions without being forced by financial pressure. It is about choice-the freedom to decide how you spend your time, where you work, and what kind of life you want to live.

At its core, financial freedom exists when your income-generating assets consistently cover your essential living expenses. These assets may include investments, rental income, dividends, business profits, or other passive income sources. When these streams are strong enough to support your lifestyle, employment becomes optional rather than compulsory. Work may continue-but by preference, not necessity.

Importantly, financial freedom looks different for everyone. For some individuals, it means retiring early and traveling the world. For others, it may mean reducing working hours to spend more time with family. Some aspire to start a passion-driven venture, engage in social impact initiatives, or pursue research and creative work without worrying about monthly bills. The definition depends on personal goals, values, and lifestyle expectations.

This is why financial planning must begin with clarity. Instead of chasing arbitrary wealth targets, individuals should calculate their annual living costs and determine the asset base required to sustain them. By aligning investments with personal aspirations, financial freedom becomes measurable and achievable.

Ultimately, financial freedom is less about luxury and more about autonomy-the power to live life on your own terms.

9.2 Calculating Your Financial Freedom Number

The financial freedom number represents the corpus required to sustain desired lifestyle expenses.
A simple approach:

1. Calculate annual essential expenses.
2. Estimate safe withdrawal rate from investments.
3. Determine the required investment corpus.

Financial freedom becomes practical only when it is quantified. The "financial freedom number" is the total investment corpus required to generate enough income to cover your desired annual expenses without relying on active employment. Instead of treating financial independence as a vague aspiration, this approach converts it into a structured, achievable target.

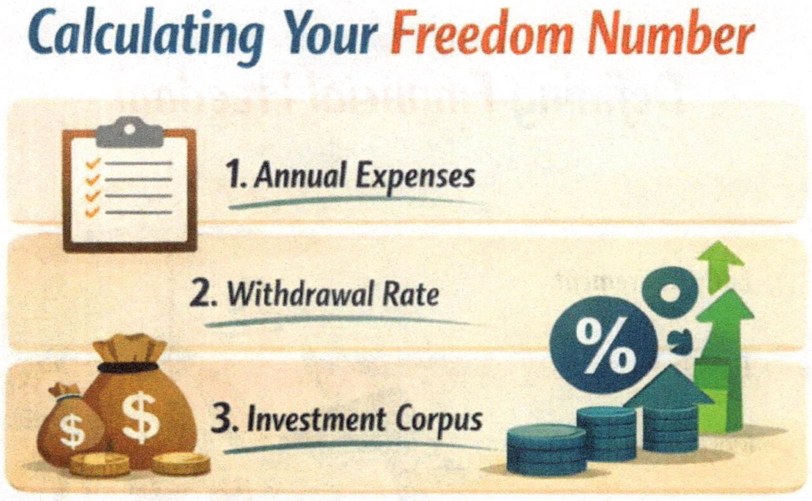

The first step is to **calculate your annual essential expenses** . This includes housing, food, utilities, healthcare, insurance, transportation, education costs, and basic lifestyle needs. It is important to be realistic-neither underestimating nor inflating expenses. Some individuals may also include discretionary spending such as travel or hobbies if those are integral to their desired lifestyle.

The second step is to **estimate a safe withdrawal rate**. This refers to the percentage of your investment portfolio that can be withdrawn annually without significantly depleting the principal over time. Conservative financial planning often uses a moderate withdrawal assumption to ensure sustainability across varying market conditions.

The third step is to **determine the required corpus** . For example, if annual expenses amount to ₹10 lakh and a conservative withdrawal rate of 4% is assumed, the required corpus would be approximately ₹2.5 crore. This is because 4% of ₹2.5 crore equals ₹10 lakh annually. While actual calculations may adjust for inflation, taxes, and asset allocation, this basic framework provides clarity.

By calculating this number, financial freedom shifts from being an emotional goal to a measurable financial milestone. Once defined, individuals can track progress, optimize savings rates, and design investment strategies that steadily move them toward independence.

Annual Essential Expenses (₹)	Assumed Safe Withdrawal Rate	Required Investment Corpus (₹)
6,00,000	4%	1,50,00,000
8,00,000	4%	2,00,00,000
10,00,000	4%	2,50,00,000
12,00,000	4%	3,00,00,000
15,00,000	4%	3,75,00,000

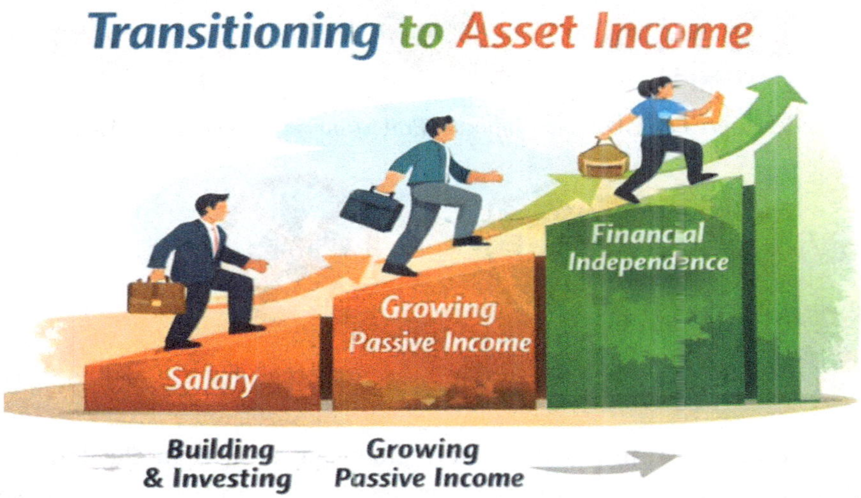

9.3 Transitioning from Active Income to Asset Income

Financial independence is achieved gradually. Income from investments begins to supplement salary, then cover partial expenses, and eventually replace earned income.

Financial independence rarely happens overnight. It is a gradual shift from relying entirely on earned income (salary or business income) to generating increasing income from assets. This transition typically unfolds in stages, requiring discipline, patience, and consistent reinvestment.

In the early years of a career, most income comes from active work. At this stage, the focus should be on building savings habits, investing systematically, and allowing compounding to begin. Contributions to diversified assets-such as equity investments, retirement funds, or income-generating property-lay the foundation for future asset income.

Over time, these investments start producing returns in the form of dividends, interest, rental income, or capital gains. Initially, this passive income may seem small compared to salary. However, as the investment base expands and earnings are reinvested, asset income begins to accelerate. The compounding effect becomes visible after years of disciplined investing.

Case Illustration:
Consider an individual who begins systematic investing at age 25. For 20 years, they allocate a portion of salary into diversified equity funds and later acquire a rental property. In the first decade, asset income is modest and largely reinvested. By their early 40s, dividends and rental earnings cover nearly 50% of annual living expenses. This reduces financial pressure and increases flexibility in career choices.

A few years later, continued reinvestment and portfolio growth allow passive income to exceed total expenses. At this stage, employment becomes optional. The individual may continue working for fulfilment, entrepreneurship, or social impact-but not out of necessity

The key insight is that asset income grows gradually and requires consistency. The earlier the transition process begins, the smoother and more sustainable financial independence becomes.

9.4 Maintaining Wealth After Achieving Freedom

Financial independence is not the end-it requires ongoing management. Portfolio rebalancing, inflation protection, and periodic review are necessary.
Wealth preservation strategies include:

- Diversified asset allocation
- Maintaining emergency reserves
- Avoiding high-risk speculation

Sustainable freedom depends on disciplined financial stewardship even after achieving independence.

Reaching financial independence is a milestone-but it is not the finish line. Once active income becomes optional, the responsibility shifts from wealth creation to wealth preservation and sustainability Without careful management, even a well-built portfolio can erode due to inflation, poor asset allocation, or emotional decision-making.

One of the most important practices after achieving freedom is **portfolio rebalancing**. Over time, certain assets may grow faster than others, changing the original risk profile of the portfolio. For example, a strong equity rally might increase stock exposure beyond the intended allocation. Periodic rebalancing restores balance, manages risk, and ensures alignment with long-term goals.

Inflation protection is equally critical. Living costs rise steadily over time, and a portfolio that only preserves capital without generating growth may gradually lose purchasing power. Maintaining a portion of growth-oriented assets-such as equities or inflation-linked instruments-helps ensure that income keeps pace with rising expenses.

Another essential safeguard is **diversified asset allocation**. Spreading investments across different asset classes reduces vulnerability to market downturns in any single sector. Diversification stabilizes income streams and protects against concentrated losses.

Maintaining **emergency reserves** remains important even after independence. Unexpected healthcare costs, economic downturns, or family obligations can arise at any stage of life. Liquidity prevents forced liquidation of long-term investments during unfavourable market conditions.

Finally, avoiding excessive risk becomes crucial. High-risk speculation may appear tempting when active income is no longer required, but large losses can jeopardize financial stability. Sustainable freedom depends on disciplined decision-making, periodic reviews, and thoughtful stewardship.

True financial freedom is not only about achieving independence-it is about preserving it responsibly for decades to come.

Strategy	Purpose	Action Required	Long-Term Benefit
Portfolio Rebalancing	Maintain desired risk level	Review allocation annually; adjust mix	Prevents overexposure to volatile assets
Diversified Asset Allocation	Reduce concentration risk	Spread across equity, debt, real assets	Stabilizes income and protects capital
Inflation Protection	Preserve purchasing power	Maintain growth-oriented investments	Ensures income keeps pace with rising costs
Emergency Reserve Maintenance	Handle unexpected expenses	Keep 6–12 months of expenses liquid	Avoids forced sale of long-term assets
Withdrawal Rate Monitoring	Sustain long-term corpus	Review annual withdrawal percentage	Prevents premature depletion of wealth
Avoiding High-Risk Speculation	Protect achieved independence	Limit exposure to speculative ventures	Reduces probability of large capital loss

References

Chapter 1: Your Money Story – Understanding Your Financial Identity

1. Kahneman, D. (2011). *Thinking, Fast and Slow.* Farrar, Straus and Giroux.
2. Thaler, R. H., & Sunstein, C. R. (2008). *Nudge: Improving Decisions About Health, Wealth, and Happiness.* Yale University Press.
3. Shefrin, H. (2002). *Beyond Greed and Fear: Understanding Behavioural Finance and the Psychology of Investing.* Oxford University Press.
4. Klontz, B., Klontz, T., & Kahler, R. (2008). *Mind Over Money.* Currency.

Chapter 2: Income Is Not Wealth – Breaking the Paycheck Illusion

1. Stanley, T. J., & Danko, W. D. (1996). *The Millionaire Next Door.* Longstreet Press.
2. Collins, J. L. (2016). *The Simple Path to Wealth.* CreateSpace Independent Publishing.
3. Piketty, T. (2014). *Capital in the Twenty-First Century.* Harvard University Press.
4. Lusardi, A., & Mitchell, O. S. (2014). "The Economic Importance of Financial Literacy." *Journal of Economic Literature,* 52(1), 5–44. https://doi.org/10.1257/jel.52.1.5

Chapter 3: Budgeting with Purpose – Designing a Money Blueprint

1. Ramsey, D. (2003). *The Total Money Makeover.* Thomas Nelson.
2. Sethi, R. (2019). *I Will Teach You to Be Rich* (2nd ed.). Workman Publishing.
3. Consumer Financial Protection Bureau (CFPB). (n.d.). *Budgeting Worksheets and Tools.* https://www.consumerfinance.gov

4. Kapoor, J. R., Dalbey, L. R., & Hughes, R. J. (2017). *Personal Finance* (12th ed.). McGraw-Hill Education.

Chapter 4: Emergency Funds & Financial Safety Nets

1. Federal Reserve Board. (2023). *Report on the Economic Well-Being of U.S. Households.* https://www.federalreserve.gov

2. Lusardi, A. (2011). "Americans' Financial Capability." *National Bureau of Economic Research Working Paper No. 17103.* https://www.nber.org/papers/w17103

3. Rejda, G. E., & McNamara, M. (2016). *Principles of Risk Management and Insurance* (12th ed.). Pearson.

4. Insurance Regulatory and Development Authority of India (IRDAI). (n.d.). Consumer education resources. https://www.irdai.gov.in

Chapter 5: The Power of Compounding – Letting Time Work for You

1. Bernstein, W. J. (2002). *The Four Pillars of Investing.* McGraw-Hill.

2. Malkiel, B. G. (2019). *A Random Walk Down Wall Street* (12th ed.). W. W. Norton & Company.

3. Bogle, J. C. (2017). *The Little Book of Common-Sense Investing.* Wiley.

4. U.S. Securities and Exchange Commission (SEC). (n.d.). *Compound Interest Calculator & Investor Education.* https://www.investor.gov

Chapter 6: Investing Basics – From Fear to Financial Confidence

1. Bodie, Z., Kane, A., & Marcus, A. J. (2021). *Investments* (12th ed.). McGraw-Hill Education.

2. Graham, B. (2006). *The Intelligent Investor* (Revised ed.). HarperBusiness.

3. CFA Institute. (2022). *Investment Foundations Program Curriculum.* https://www.cfainstitute.org

Chapter 7: Multiple Streams of Income – Making Money Multiply

1. Kiyosaki, R. T. (2017). *Rich Dad Poor Dad.* Plata Publishing.
2. Ferriss, T. (2007). *The 4-Hour Workweek.* Crown Publishing.
3. Damodaran, A. (2012). *Investment Valuation* (3rd ed.). Wiley.
4. International Monetary Fund (IMF). (2022). *Global Financial Stability Report.* https://www.imf.org

Chapter 8: Smart Tax Planning & Wealth Protection

1. Internal Revenue Service (IRS). (n.d.). *Tax Guide for Individuals.* https://www.irs.gov

   Black, K., & Skipper, H. (2000). *Life Insurance* (13th ed.). Prentice Hall.

2. Sitkoff, R. H., & Dukeminier, J. (2017). *Wills, Trusts, and Estates* (10th ed.). Wolters Kluwer.

Chapter 9: Financial Freedom Blueprint – Designing Your Exit Strategy

1. FIRE Movement overview – Hester, V. R. (2018). *Financial Freedom.* Portfolio.
2. Cooley, P. L., Hubbard, C. M., & Walz, D. T. (1998). "Retirement Savings: Choosing a Withdrawal Rate That Is Sustainable." *AAII Journal.*
3. Milevsky, M. A. (2012). *The 7 Most Important Equations for Your Retirement.* Wiley.

Appendix

1. Glossary of Key Terms

Asset – A resource that generates income or appreciates in value over time.

Liability – An obligation or expense that reduces financial value.

Compounding – The process where earnings generate additional earnings through reinvestment.

Cash Flow – The movement of money into and out of an individual's finances.

Diversification – Spreading investments across asset types to reduce risk.

Emergency Fund – Liquid savings set aside for unexpected financial needs.

Passive Income – Earnings generated with minimal ongoing effort after initial setup.

Active Income – Income earned through direct effort such as salary or professional services.

Asset Allocation – Distribution of investments across different asset classes.

Risk Tolerance – An individual's ability and willingness to endure market fluctuations.

Liquidity – The ease with which an asset can be converted into cash.

Inflation – The rate at which purchasing power decreases over time.

Lifestyle Inflation – Increased spending as income rises.

Net Worth – Total assets minus total liabilities.

Financial Freedom Number – The investment corpus required to sustain lifestyle expenses through passive income.

2. Data Sources and Datasets

The following institutional sources provide credible financial data, market insights, and economic indicators:

Global Sources

- World Bank Open Data – https://data.worldbank.org
- International Monetary Fund (IMF) Data Portal – https://www.imf.org
- OECD Data – https://data.oecd.org
- Federal Reserve Economic Data (FRED) – https://fred.stlouisfed.org

India-Specific Sources

- Reserve Bank of India (RBI) Database on Indian Economy – https://dbie.rbi.org.in
- Securities and Exchange Board of India (SEBI) Reports – https://www.sebi.gov.in
- National Stock Exchange (NSE) Historical Data – https://www.nseindia.com
- Bombay Stock Exchange (BSE) Market Data – https://www.bseindia.com
- Income Tax Department of India – https://www.incometax.gov.in

Financial Literacy & Consumer Behaviour

- OECD Financial Literacy Surveys
- World Bank Global Findex Database
- National Bureau of Economic Research (NBER) Working Papers

3. Tools and Frameworks

This book integrates practical tools and strategic financial frameworks for real-world implementation.

Budgeting Frameworks

- 50–30–20 Rule
- Zero-Based Budgeting
- Envelope Allocation Method

Investment Frameworks

- Strategic Asset Allocation Model
- Risk–Return Matrix
- Diversification Grid
- Systematic Investment Plan (SIP) Strategy

Wealth Protection Framework

- Emergency Fund Laddering
- Insurance Coverage Mapping
- Estate Planning Checklist

Financial Freedom Framework

- Annual Expense Multiplier Model
- Safe Withdrawal Rate Concept
- Passive Income Ratio Calculation

Digital Tools

- Personal finance tracking apps
- Online compound interest calculators
- Retirement corpus planners
- Tax planning simulators

4. References for Further Reading

Foundational Books

- Kahneman, D. *Thinking, Fast and Slow*
- Bogle, J. C. *The Little Book of Common-Sense Investing*
- Graham, B. *The Intelligent Investor*
- Stanley, T. J., & Danko, W. D. *The Millionaire Next Door*
- Malkiel, B. G. *A Random Walk Down Wall Street*

Academic & Institutional Resources

- CFA Institute Investment Foundations Program
- OECD Financial Education Reports
- World Bank Pension and Retirement Studies
- Federal Reserve Household Economic Well-Being Reports

These resources offer deeper academic and practical understanding of behavioural finance, investment strategy, and retirement planning.

5. Future Directions in Personal Finance and Wealth Creation

The financial landscape is rapidly evolving. Emerging trends will shape the next generation of wealth-building strategies:

Digital Investing & FinTech Integration

Robo-advisors, algorithm-driven portfolios, and AI-powered financial planning are simplifying access to markets.

Sustainable & ESG Investing

Investors increasingly align portfolios with environmental, social, and governance values.

Decentralized Finance (DeFi)

Blockchain-based systems are redefining lending, investing, and asset ownership.

Personalized Financial Analytics

Data-driven insights will enable highly customized budgeting and investment plans.

Financial Literacy Expansion

Governments and institutions are prioritizing financial education to reduce economic inequality.

The future belongs to financially informed individuals who combine technology with disciplined strategy.

6. Summary of Key Points

- Wealth begins with understanding your financial mindset.
- Income alone does not guarantee financial security.
- Budgeting creates clarity and control.
- Emergency funds and insurance protect progress.
- Compounding rewards consistency and patience
- Diversified investing reduces risk and builds confidence.
- Multiple income streams enhance stability.
- Tax planning preserves accumulated wealth.
- Financial freedom is a measurable, achievable goal.

ABOUT THE AUTHORS

Prof. Dr. Punit Goel is a distinguished academician, prolific author, and research mentor with more than 32 years of experience in teaching, research, and academic leadership. He currently serves as Professor and Editor-in-Chief of MIJCATR at Maharaja Agrasen Himalayan Garhwal University, where he actively promotes research quality and scholarly innovation. He earned his Ph.D. from Gurukula Kangri Vishwavidyalaya with doctoral research focused on Performance Management Systems in IT companies.

An exceptionally productive scholar, Prof. Goel has authored 85 books and published over 350 research papers in reputed Scopus, IEEE, and other peer-reviewed journals. He has successfully guided multiple Ph.D. scholars, with several awarded under his supervision, and is presently mentoring eight research candidates. He serves on the editorial boards of more than 20 international journals and holds over 30 patents. Notably, he is a world record holder for publishing the maximum number of physical and e-books on a single day, reflecting his extraordinary academic dedication and publishing excellence.

Niharika Singh is an innovation-driven researcher and Computer Science engineer dedicated to building secure, scalable, and ethically grounded digital ecosystems. With a strong foundation in Computer Science and Data Science, she focuses on solving real-world challenges through applied research in artificial intelligence, optimization techniques, and resilient infrastructure design. She is the author and co-author of over 20 IEEE-indexed conference papers and journal publications, contributing to areas such as AI-based optimization, blockchain-enabled voting systems, cloud robustness, and intelligent business process automation.

Remarkably, by the age of 21, Niharika has authored and co-authored 52 books, earning recognition as one of the youngest world record holders for the maximum number of books published on a single day. She is also the author of the bestselling novel Kali Ghata, a powerful narrative portraying the life struggles of an Indian girl. Positioned at the intersection of emerging technologies and applied innovation, Niharika is committed to advancing secure, trustworthy, and sustainable next-generation systems.

Dr. Subodh Sachan is a distinguished logistics leader with nearly three decades of expertise in global freight forwarding, customs operations, and integrated supply chain management. As the CEO of Masters Logistics Solutions India Pvt. Ltd. (MLSIPL), he transformed the company from a promising 2014 startup into a nationally recognized logistics powerhouse trusted by leading international brands. His leadership reflects innovation, empathy, and strategic resilience, earning him deep respect across the logistics industry.

A strong advocate of transparency, corporate governance, and sustainability, he has spearheaded digital transformation and environmentally responsible initiatives within MLSIPL. Under his stewardship, the company has received prestigious honors including the India Cargo Awards, ET Leadership Excellence Award, CII SCALE National Award, and Cargo NXT Award. Dr. Sachan is also a prolific author of 52 books and holds a world record for publishing the maximum number of physical and e-books on a single day.

Dr. K. Yogesh is a distinguished educationist, researcher, and prolific author with a strong academic foundation, holding M.Com, M.A. (Economics), M.A. (Education), and a Ph.D. in Commerce. He is UGC NET-qualified in both Commerce and Education. As the Chairman of Socrates Social Research University and NASA Trust, New Delhi, he provides visionary leadership in higher education and research advancement. He is also the Founder of Gyan Sagar Education Society, contributing significantly to academic development and social initiatives.

Dr. Yogesh has actively participated in numerous international conferences and has honoured over 500 eminent personalities in India through SSRU initiatives. A member of prestigious organizations including Vishva Yuvak Kendra, International Youth Hostel, Scindia Club of India, Lion's Club of India, and IMC Chamber of Commerce and Industry, he has authored 63 books and holds a world record for publishing the maximum number of physical and e-books on a single day.

15. Librerías Gandhi– Mexico
16. Google Book – United States
17. Google Audio Book – United States
18. Indigo – Canada
19. Kobo – Canada
20. Kindle – United States
21. Lafeltrinelli – Italy
22. Lehmanns – Germany
23. Lulu – United States
24. Morawa – Austria
25. Rakuten Japan – Japan (Rakuten)
26. Smashwords – United States
27. Tolino / Thalia – Germany
28. Vivlio – France
29. Saxo – Denmark
30. Yes24 – South Korea And Others.

Additional Benefits:

- Your book will be available on 30+ major platforms worldwide, increasing visibility and accessibility.
- You will also receive five book reviews , including:
    - Three reviews from distinguished university professors.
    - Two reviews from colleagues, senior peers or mentors.

Take a step toward global recognition by publishing with WISSIRA Press.

www.books.wissira.us

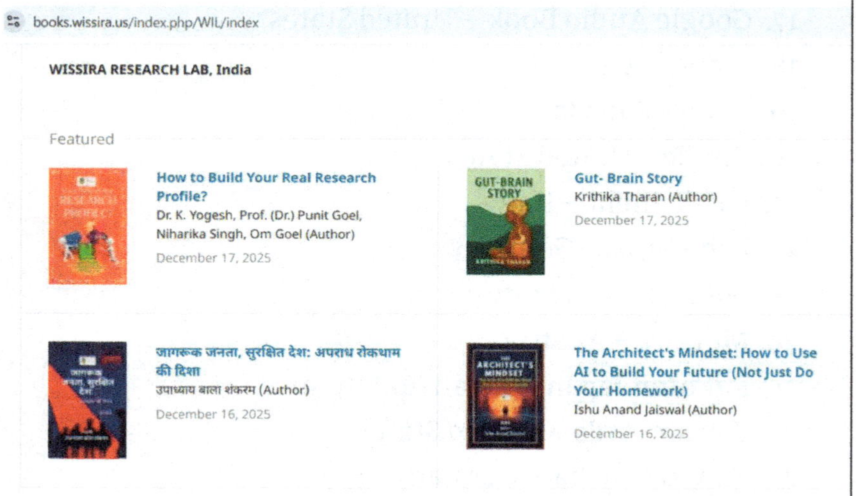

www.books.wissira.us

DOI: https://doi.org/10.63345/book.wrl.2512000324

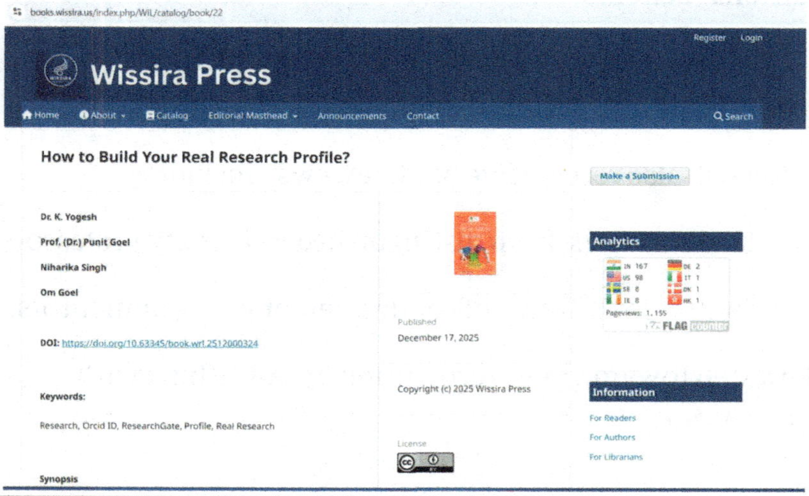

Let’s Manage Your Hard-Earned Money: Give it Permission to Earn for You Now

https://books.wissira.us/index.php/WIL/login

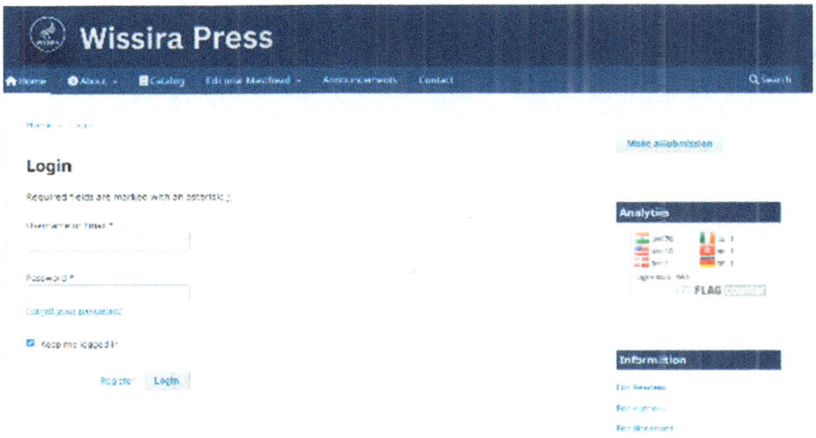

https://books.wissira.us/index.php/WIL/catalog

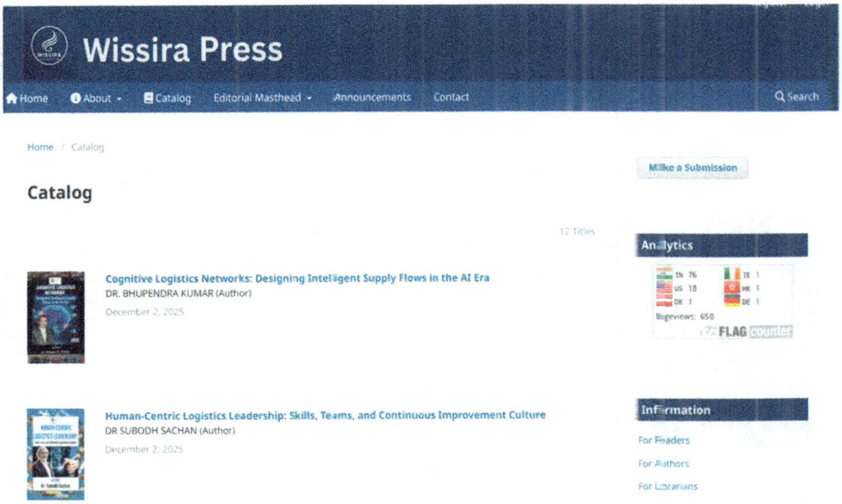

https://books.wissira.us/index.php/WIL/about/contact

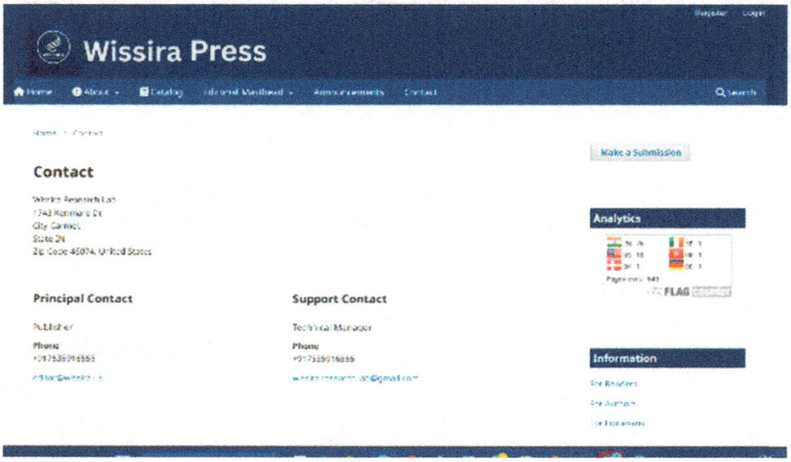

https://www.amazon.in/dp/B0G7MQFD2L

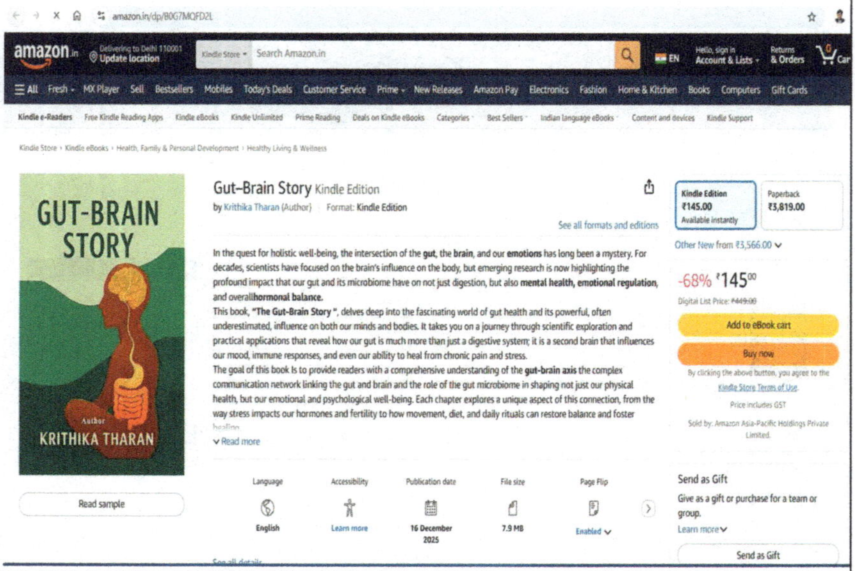

https://books.apple.com/us/book/the-architects-mindset-how-to-use-ai-to-build-your/id6756545876

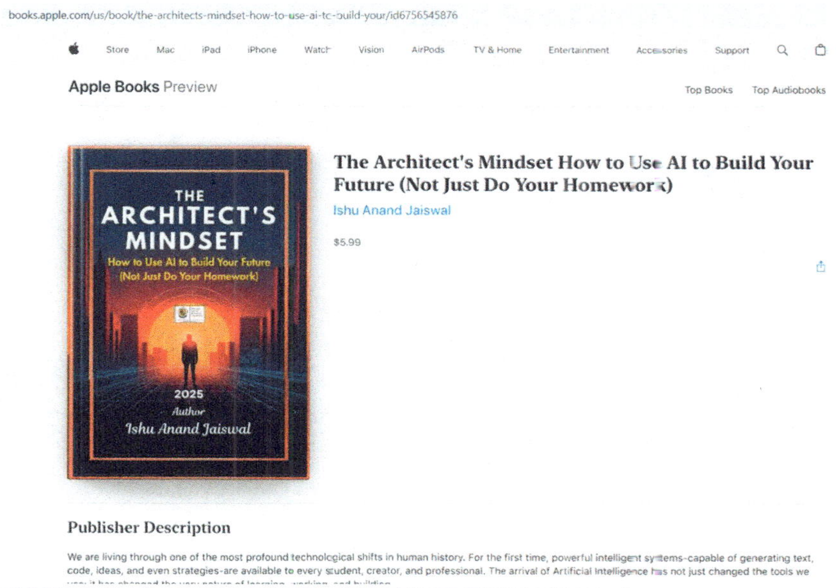

Flipkart:

https://tinyurl.com/WissieaPressBook250306Human

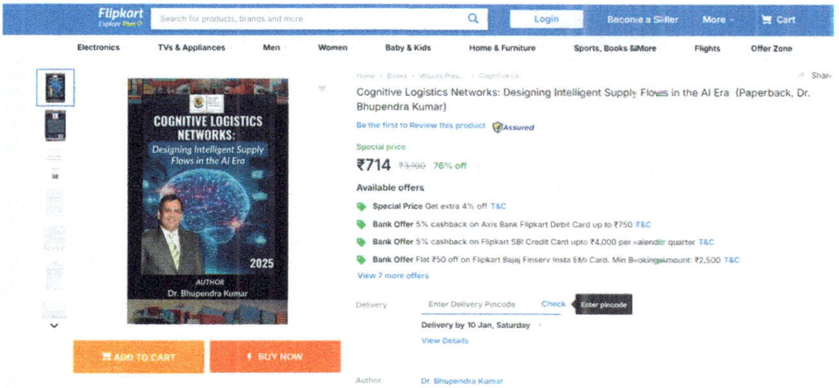

https://tinyurl.com/WRLVivlioBooks

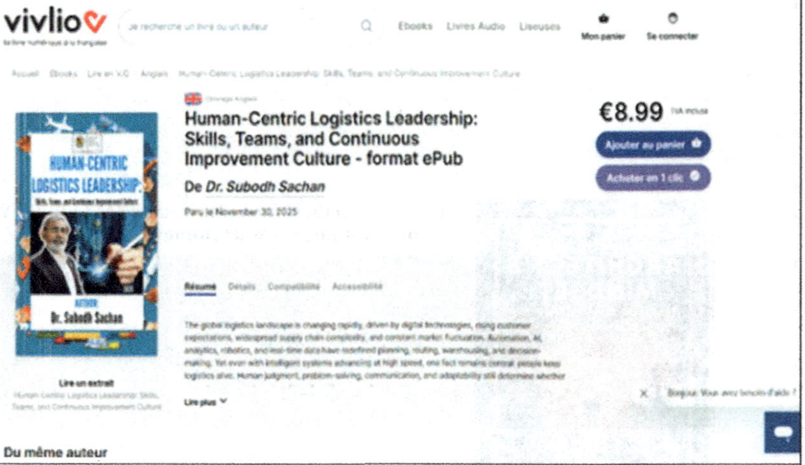

https://fable.co/book/x-9798230804772

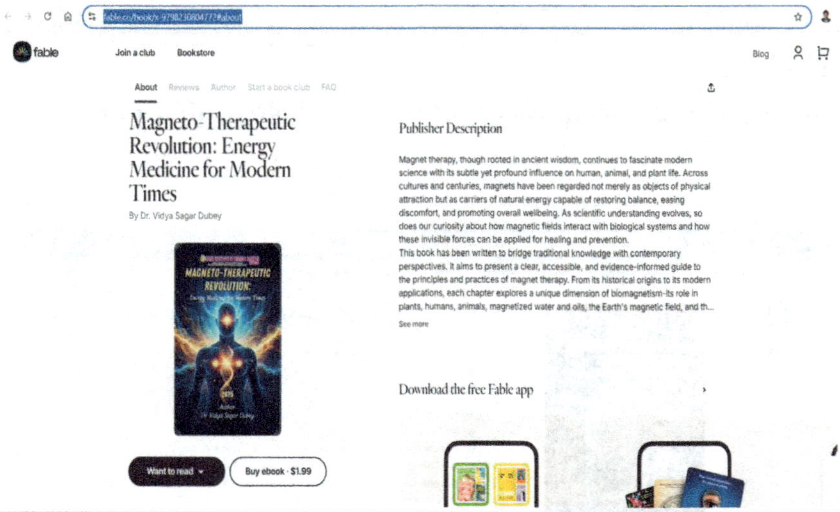

https://tinyurl.com/WRLKoboBooks

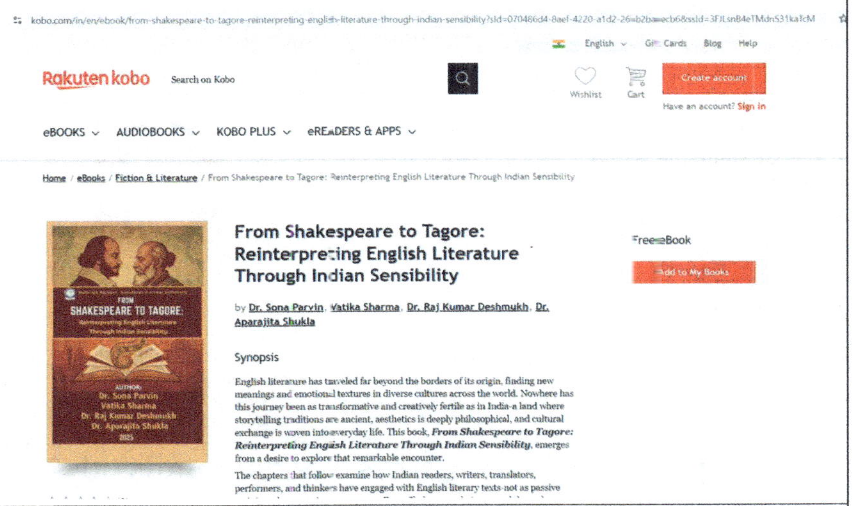

https://tinyurl.com/WRLLuluBooks

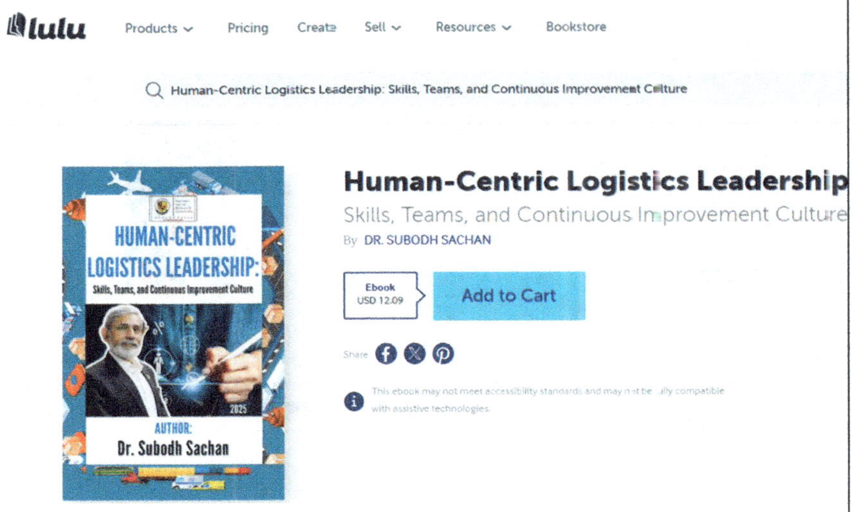

https://play.google.com/store/audiobooks/details?id=AQAAAEDqoRHh6M

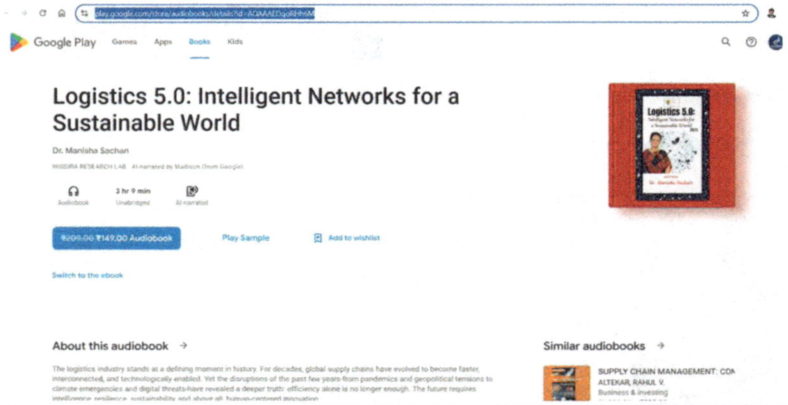

https://play.google.com/store/books/details?id=TbmfEQAAQBAJ

Amazon Kindle

Amazon

Flipkart

LULU

Apple Books

Barnes & Nobles

Everand

Fable

Kobo

Analytics

IN	135	IT	1
US	84	DK	1
SE	8	HK	1
IE	8	DE	1

Pageviews: 1,012

FLAG counter

Information

For Readers

For Authors

For Librarians

Keywords

sustain long-term operational excellence.

Across the nine chapters of this work, readers will find a structured and practical approach to understanding how leadership influences logistics outcomes. Beginning with the foundations of human-centric leadership, the book explores essential competencies such as communication, empathy, decision-making, and ethical responsibility-skills that enable leaders to build credibility and trust in high-pressure environments. It then moves deeper into the dynamics of teamwork, motivation, and empowerment, highlighting how resilient and collaborative teams become the backbone of

Smashwords

Tolino

Vivlio

Google Books

WORLD RECORDS BOOK OF INDIA

Certificate

HIGHEST NUMBER OF BOOKS LAUNCHED SIMULTANEOUSLY IN DUAL-FORMAT IN A SINGLE DAY

This is to certify that **Prof. Dr. PUNIT GOEL, Er. NIHARIKA SINGH, Dr. SUBODH SACHAN** and **Dr. K YOGESH,** achieved a remarkable publishing milestone by jointly launching **51 Books on a Single day,** released in both e-copy and printed formats and set a new World Record on 8th Mar 2026 at India International Centre, Lodhi Road, New Delhi. 51 Books was published by Wissira Research Lab, USA ensuring formal recognition, authenticity and global discoverability across international publishing and library systems. It's simultaneous dual-format launch of all titles, reflecting meticulous planning, editorial rigor and excellence in modern publishing workflows across both physical and digital platforms.

WRBI: 1386 - 2026
Date : 08-03-2026

In Association with

Sushma Narvekar
Sushma Narvekar
Chief Editor-World Records Book of India

www.worldrecordsbookofindia.com / www.sanjeevanisocialfoundation.org

Made in the USA
Monee, IL
02 November 2026

67380085R00072